INSIDE
SOUTH AUSTIN

South Austin

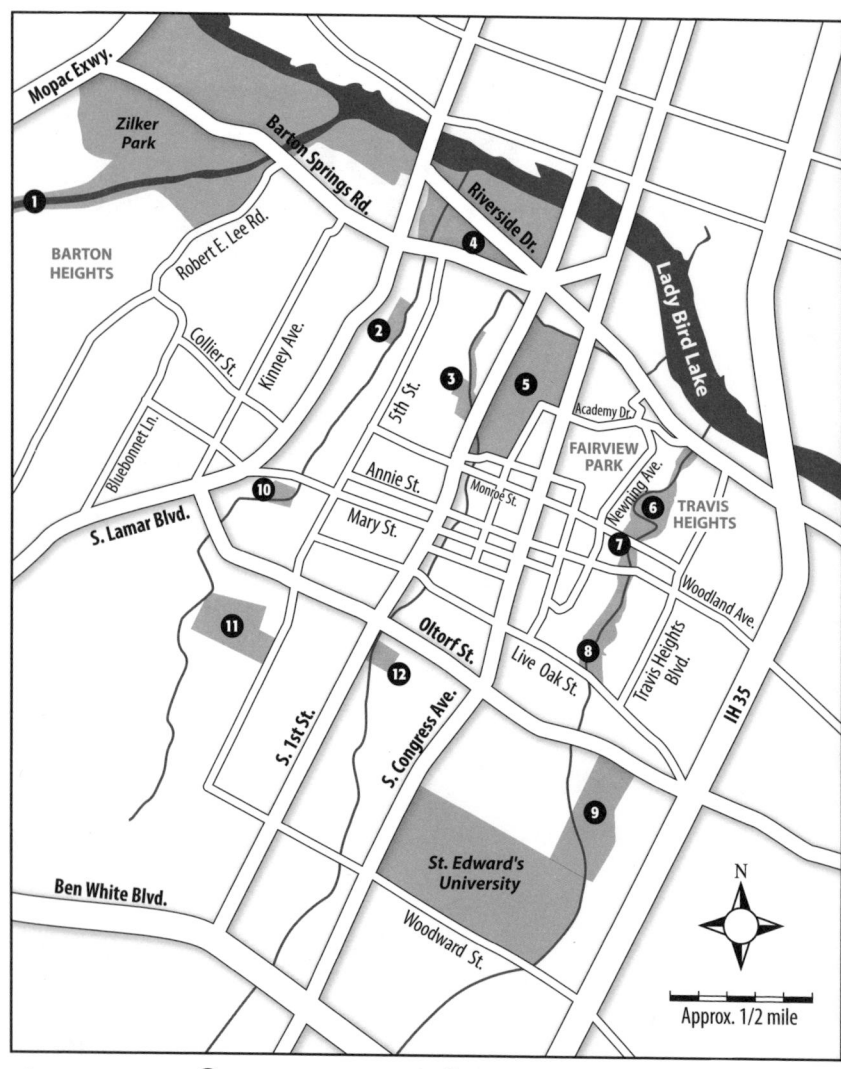

Approx. 1/2 mile

INSIDE
SOUTH AUSTIN
A GUIDE

DIANE BARNET

MAVERICK PUBLISHING COMPANY

Library of Congress Cataloging-in-Publication Data

Barnet, Diane.
  Inside South Austin : a guide / Diane Barnet
    p. cm.
  Includes bibliographical references and index.
  ISBN 978-1-893271-50-0 (alk. paper)
1. South Austin (Austin, Tex.)–Guidebooks. 2. South Austin (Austin, Tex.)–History.
3. Austin (Tex.)–Guidebooks. 4. Austin (Tex.)–History. I. Title.
  F394.A96S684 2009
  917.64'31–dc22

                                    2009020299

10 9 8 7 6 5 4 3 2 1

Cover, book design and electronic publishing — Nio Graphics, Inc. and Kell Creative, LLC.
Frontispiece map by Leslie Kell.

CONTENTS

SO CLOSE YET SO FAR OUT

Paris has its Left Bank, New York City its Greenwich Village, San Francisco its North Beach. Austin has South Austin.

Austin is the capital of Texas and home to the University of Texas. As state government and the university expanded, Austin's population grew from 50,000 in the 1930s to 175,000 thirty years later. Arrival of high-tech companies in the 1970s has since quadrupled that number, to beyond 700,000. Almost everything of political and financial importance in Austin still happens north of the Lower Colorado River, dammed to form Lady Bird Lake, formerly Town Lake.

South Austin goes its own way. Well within Austin city limits, it covers some nine square miles, bordered generally on the west by Zilker Park, on the south by Ben White Boulevard and on the east by IH 35. Its population, slowly growing, is close to 45,000. Creasing South Austin's rolling, tree-studded terrain are the deep ravines of four creeks running northward into the Colorado River: Barton, West Bouldin, East Bouldin and Blunn.

Even though South Austin has undergone many changes in the last decade or two, the Colorado still separates two distinctive communities, linked by three bridges: South Lamar Boulevard, South First Street and South Congress Avenue, a bridge now named in memory of Ann W. Richards, Texas governor in 1990–94 that draws national attention. A colony of Mexican free-tailed bats that began forming under the bridge in 1980 now numbers 1.5 million, the largest urban bat colony in North America. Each summer evening the bats—which fly up from Mexico in March and April and return in October for the winter—set out at dusk to devour up to 30,000 pounds of insects. Hordes of Austinites celebrate the spectacle with a Bat Fest each August.

South Austin was a blue-collar, semi-rural backwater until the 1950s. An influx of rednecks and hippies, many of them objecting to the Vietnam

War, began stirring the dust in the late 1960s and early '70s, led by Willie Nelson, who brought his outlaw country music to Austin and settled down. Stuffier denizens of such genteel neighborhoods as Tarrytown, Mount Bonnell, Hyde Park and Northwest Hills—all north of the river—curled a lip at South Austin.

Diners, cafés, bars and Mexican joints blossomed, cooking some of the best food around. The Armadillo World Headquarters near the corner of Barton Springs Road and Riverside Drive offered definitive psychedelic, rock and country sounds. The Continental Club, the Broken Spoke and the Saxon Pub paved the way for dozens of vibrant music venues. Vintage clothing shops like Lucy in Disguise With Diamonds, Flashback and Flipnotics appeared; many still flourish.

South Austin was livable, tolerant and rich in functional neighborhoods, as well as being laid-back, funky and eclectic. Bikers lived next door to bohemian artists and writers. Students, Hispanic families and aspiring musicians existed harmoniously kitty-corner from grizzled old-timers. The slow pace, cheap rents and minimal zoning laws allowed creativity of all sorts to flourish. Houses with mauve trim, front-yard sculptures made of hubcaps, wire coils and old weathervanes, cats, chickens, even a solitary goat tethered in a Mary Street front yard, all found acceptance in South Austin. They were just part of the landscape.

Housing stock, much of it dating from the 1940s, '30s and earlier, ran to small frame bungalows with gingerbread trim, tiny stucco haciendas painted chartreuse or pink and fieldstone cottages with overgrown backyards. The

One of the most memorable vistas in Texas is down South Austin's South Congress Avenue to the state capitol nearly two miles away.

narrow streets were overhung with lush oaks, cottonwoods, magnolias and palms—a fragile environment for a region ripe for invasion by expanding downtown Austin.

In the 1980s battle lines began to be drawn.

In the middle of the decade, the Austin city council planned to widen South Lamar and add a median strip. Danny Young, then owner of the Texicali Grill and known unofficially as "the mayor of South Austin," started a vigorous campaign to rally local merchants against the plan. The widening was quashed. "In South Austin, we do things the way we want," Young was quoted as saying, "and we hope that you like it. But if you don't, we'll do it anyway."

In 1981 the proposed construction of the low-rise 63-unit Ashton Green Condominiums on Kinney Avenue sparked the founding of the Zilker Neighborhood Association to fight the construction. Nevertheless, the condos were built two years later. But relatively little development occurred in the area over the next decade and a half, with the major exception of a complex at Barton Springs Road and South Lamar Boulevard.

South Austin's attitude is captured on the sign of South Congress Avenue's Austin Motel, family owned for more than seventy years.

The broadening appeal of South Austin made it profitable to capitalize on the area's charm. The once respectable Austin Motel in the 1200 block of South Congress Avenue, family-owned since 1938, had become rundown. In 1993 a younger member of the family, Dottye Dean, restored the motel to its original classic cozy style, with forty-one rooms and a sign that speaks for old South Austin as it quips "So close yet so far out."

Next door, the Spanish-style San José Motel opened in 1939 as "an ultra modern tourist court," but it had evolved into a haven for drug users. Austin attorney Liz Lambert bought the complex in 1995, hired San Antonio's Lake/Flato architects and began a $3 million renovation into the

Among South Austin's bucolic recreation spots is the mouth of Barton Creek on Lady Bird Lake.

compact and well-appointed Hotel San José, completed three years later and including two courtyards and cactus and sagebrush landscaping.

South Austin made the big screen. In 1991 Austin film director Richard Linklater filmed Slacker partly in South Austin. Writer Mike Judge, creator of television's *Beavis and Butthead* and *King of the Hill,* set the latter in fictional Arlen, Texas, based partly on working-class South Austin.

South Austin had a higher pickup-to-SUV ratio than other residential areas of the city, not to mention the biggest concentration of non-power push mowers. A plethora of bumper stickers proclaimed "South Austin: We're All Here 'Cause We're Not All There," "South Austin: Secede," "78704–More Than A Zip Code, A State Of Mind," "78704–A Way Of Life" and "7870Forever–South Austin, Texas, Earth."

Other bumper stickers owed their existence to Austin Community College librarian Red Wassenich, who in 2000 called KOOP radio during its fund drive to make a contribution. When asked why he felt compelled to help, he replied that he wanted to "keep Austin weird."

It soon occurred to Wassenich that this phrase made a good slogan. He and his wife began to produce T-shirts and bumper stickers for sale. Places like Boulder, Colorado, and Santa Cruz, California, picked up the sentiment in their own bumper stickers.

By the beginning of the millennium, growth pressures spurred by Austin's booming high-tech economy began seriously spilling over into South Austin. The number of high-rise condominium developments surged past two dozen before the end of the decade. Modest older homes were increasingly being replaced by larger single-family or multi-family projects that jarred the character of the neighborhoods. Such change was mitigated throughout the city in 2006, when Austin's city council passed a "McMansion" ordinance restricting the size and character of new single-family homes and duplexes in six zones and forty-eight neighborhoods.

But change continued to creep, and South Austin residents struggled to adjust. "It's gone from a blue-collar to a no-collar neighborhood," opined Austin American-Statesman columnist, writer and long-time South Austinite John Kelso. "There's been more change in the last two years than in the preceding twenty-nine years I've lived here." Former Bouldin Creek Neighborhood Association president Sean Kelly cited threats posed by stratospheric property taxes, land speculation and destruction of older homes to the South Austin way of life. "South Austin," he declared, "is too cool to bulldoze."

Preservation of South Austin's character began being advocated more formally—and with some success—by the Zilker and South River City Citizens neighborhood associations and by other associations promoting the South Lamar Combined Neighborhood Plan: South Lamar, Bouldin Creek, Galindo Elementary and Barton Hills/Barton View.

High-rises, traffic congestion, trendy restaurants and chic, cookie-cutter affluence, lofts and lattes may have made some inroads into the ambling streets and lanes and added contrast to the laid-back cafes that lent South Austin its old character. But there's still a lot of uniqueness in South Austin—old and new—especially if you know where to look.

One wall of a temporary building becomes a billboard while housing a sales office for a condominium complex around the historic Paggi House near Zilker Park.

2

NEIGHBORHOODS STYLISH AND WEIRD

Long ago, as the threat of Indian raids in South Austin diminished, log houses began going up, followed by frame and brick homes. Eventually, more socially elite families began clustering east of South Congress Avenue in the area now known as Travis Heights. In 1848 Sterling R. Goodrich used handmade bricks to build a one-story plantation house overlooking the Colorado at what is now 200 Lee Barton Dr., near the intersection of South Riverside Drive and South Lamar Boulevard. Later purchased and enlarged by the Italian immigrant and architect Michael Paggi, whose enterprises included a wagon business and a bathhouse at Barton Springs, the home has been restored as the **Paggi House** restaurant.

Soon elegant homes began joining the scattered farmhouses. In 1871 Daniel Perry Kinney built Rocky Cliff, a house south of Barton Springs Road on what is now Barton Boulevard. In 1875 Col. Sterling Goodrich's daughter and her husband built a house just off Kinney Avenue on property previously owned by the Raymonds, Swishers and Bouldins. Made of stone quarried at Oak Hill, the two-story house included four fireplaces and a large two-story front gallery. Its massive walls were 22 inches thick for insulation, and it held a 50-foot-deep cistern. Variously known as the

The Paggi House, now a restaurant, was built overlooking the Colorado River with handmade bricks in 1848.

Kinney Homestead, Davis Homestead or Wisteria, it stands at what is now 1610 Virginia Ave. It was acquired with eight acres of land in 1916 by George Kinney, son of pioneer Daniel Perry Kinney. The house later passed to other owners and was purchased in 1966 by Cater Joseph, whose grandfather emigrated from Lebanon to Texas in 1890 and operated a dry goods and grocery store in downtown Austin.

Swisher Addition

Open land began disappearing beneath subdivisions. In 1877 John Milton Swisher, son of pioneer James Swisher, subdivided twenty-three acres of the family farm along the San Antonio road and named streets for family members—Mary, Elizabeth, Annie, Johanna, Eva, Nellie, Monroe, Brackenridge, James, Newton. He left San Antonio Road, beginning to be known as South Congress Avenue, as it was, keeping it in direct alignment with Congress Avenue downtown and preserving an unobstructed view of the Capitol, one of the finest vistas in Texas. Swisher also ran a stagecoach line that left for San Antonio from his south bank ferry landing, charging $10 for a one-way passage. An auditor and banker as well, he organized and served as president of the stock company that eventually built Austin's street railway system.

At 1700 Newton St. is the frame **Goodwill Baptist Church.** Across the street at 1711 is **St. Annie African Methodist Episcopal Church,** its cornerstone laid in 1915. A parsonage was added in 1944. The substantial stone **Stanley House** at 1811 Newton St. was built by Robert S. Stanley in 1895 and is one of Austin's few early structures to have an excavated basement. Four pot-bellied stoves originally heated the house, which was wired for electricity in 1920. Stanley, who ran a general store around the corner in what is now the Herb Bar, was an active member at St. Annie.

The Stanley House, built in 1895, was originally heated by four pot-bellied stoves.

Emmett Shelton, an Austin memoirist born in 1905 at 211 Live Oak St., remembered that Live Oak originally did not cross Bouldin Creek. Indeed, the creek was impassible much of the time, limiting access to nearby streets. Mary Street was South Austin's main east-west artery when Shelton was growing up, and he remembered that his middle-class family never locked the doors. Living without electricity or running water, they scrubbed the laundry in cast-iron kettles with soap made from lye and ash and used oil lamps for light.

Below Bouldin Creek, between South Congress Avenue and South First Street, is the 57-acre campus of the **Texas School for the Deaf.** In 1856 Gov. Elisha M. Pease appointed a board of five trustees to find the site. Inhabitants, like those of poor farms, orphanages and state schools, were expected to benefit from fresh air and country living. Referred to then as the Deaf School or the Deaf and Dumb Asylum, the institution got its first three students in 1857. During the Civil War, when there was no money for teachers' salaries, staff members sold their own vegetables and spun wool for clothing from their flocks of sheep. A number of Victorian Gothic buildings were added as the school expanded steadily.

Fairview Park

In 1880 Gen. William Harwood Stacy, who commanded the Texas National Guard, formed a partnership with George Warner and Charles Newning, an agent for a New York bank, purchasing 200 acres between South Congress Avenue and Blunn Creek, east of the Swisher subdivision. Named Fairview Park, it became South Austin's first thoroughly planned subdivision, an upscale, owner-occupied "garden suburb" with irregularly shaped lots in a hilly area with two creeks. Stacy promoted Fairview Park as having bracing air, scenery, roads, sewers and a baseball club.

In 1888 Fairview Park developer Gen. William Harwood Stacy built this house, now the Hotel Saint Cecelia.

By 1900 a number of large Victorian homes had been built on Fairview Park lots, notably the **Stacy House** at 1201 Travis Heights Blvd., the Warner-Lucas House at 303 Academy Dr., the **Dumble-Boatright House** at 1419 Newning Ave. and the **Red-Purcell House** at 210 Academy Dr.

In 1888 Stacy built a New Orleans–style home for Henry W. Dodge. In 1900 the home was bought by Charles Miller for $1,800 at a courthouse auction. In more recent years it was a bed-and-breakfast. Since January 2009 the home and nearby bungalows, at 112 Academy Dr., have enjoyed a new incarnation as the fourteen-room **Hotel Saint Cecelia,** creatively made over by Liz Lambert, already well-known for her stunning makeovers of the Hotel San José and Marfa's Thunderbird Hotel.

In 1890 Myron D. Mather, president of the Austin Water, Light and Power Company, built the **Mather-Kirkland House,** also called the Academy, on ten acres at 402 Academy Dr. Three stories high and 4,000 square feet, the home's lower floors were made of granite remaining from the 1888 Texas State Capitol construction downtown. The house had an elaborately shingled slate roof and a panoramic view of the city across the river. In 1920 W. L. Dorsey bought the property and operated it for years as the Austin Military School for young men between the ages of 10 and 20 from "good" families. The Mather House was the main building while several other large houses in the neighborhood made up the campus.

Granite blocks left over from construction of the Texas capitol were used in 1890 for the first floor of the Mather-Kirkland House, also known as the Academy for being the onetime home of the Austin Military School.

Development in Fairview Park was disappointingly slow. By 1910 sparse construction forced the developers to subdivide the lots into smaller parcels; basic bungalows and cottages soon appeared, often with gabled or hipped roofs and deep porches. The **Brunson House** at 200 The Circle is typical of Fairview Park's early 20th-century bungalows, many showing Craftsman or Prairie School influence.

Travis Heights

In 1913 Fairview Park developer William Stacy formed the Stacy-Robbins Company with investor R. Brown Robbins. Stacy began to construct homes east of Fairview Park in a development called Travis Heights, bounded by Riverside Drive on the north, Oltorf Street on the south and on the east by today's IH-35, which cut through the northeast corner of Travis Heights. He mixed streets in a traditional grid pattern with curving avenues winding through the hilly landscape, promoting the area as a gently rolling bluff "which cannot be surpassed in beauty, convenience and healthfulness." The company ran streetcars for prospective buyers from the Capitol to Travis Heights Boulevard and even gave Ford Touring Cars as prizes.

"It is a real residence community," advertisements for Travis Heights rhapsodized in 1918, "one with a soul, the realization of a purpose, where homes are homes, not mere houses."

Stacy incorporated deed restrictions on multi-family and commercial uses to ensure that the area remained upscale. Beside Blunn Creek on the boundary with his earlier Fairview Park development he donated land for Stacy Park, with two pools, Little Stacy and the spring-fed Big Stacy. Northeast of Riverside Drive and IH-35, the newer **Norwood Park** eventually would become Austin's first dog-friendly, leash-free park.

By the time of General Stacy's death in 1928, some 600 lots had been sold and 160 homes built. His sons Harwood, Gillespie and Franklin continued to develop Travis Heights with modest bungalows in Colonial, Tudor and Spanish Colonial style up to World War II. With postwar expansion the area became more heterogeneous. It remains one of the most desirable addresses in Austin and is home to approximately 3,000 residents.

The South River City Citizens neighborhood association is seeking to have the heart of the area listed as both an Austin Local Historic District and a National Register Historic District, to preserve its ambience and slow teardowns and subsequent construction of McMansions, condos and apartment complexes. "Save Our Houses" signs dot many streets.

Oak trees shade the restored bungalows lining streets along the rolling hillsides of Travis Heights.

South of Travis Heights, at 3001 S. Congress Ave., is South Austin's largest institution, **St. Edward's University,** which has a student body of 5,300. James and Mary Doyle left most of their 500-acre cotton farm to the Roman Catholic Church. On the farmland the Holy Cross Fathers founded St. Edward's Academy in 1878, five years before the University of Texas was established. Classes were held in a makeshift building, where three farm boys formed the student body the first year. St. Edward's was chartered as a college in 1885. Its imposing Victorian Gothic style Main Building, built in 1885 and designed by the noted Galveston architect Nicholas Clayton, stands on high ground that provides a sweeping view of central Austin across the river. In 1903 a fire destroyed much of Main Building, and in 1922 the rebuilt structure sustained tornado damage. St. Edward's received its university charter in 1925. Women first arrived in 1966 as students at Maryhill College, but four years later St. Edward's became co-educational and absorbed Maryhill.

West of South First Street

While South Austin's most significant residential development around the turn of the twentieth century was happening east of South First Street, there were several notable if lesser developments to the west: the Bouldin and Dawson additions, South Heights and Evergreen Heights.

The plantation of another early settler, Col. James Bouldin, who came from Virginia in the 1850s, stretched from the river to present-day William Cannon Boulevard. After Bouldin died in 1876, his son began selling off land in what was called the Bouldin Addition, bounded by Elizabeth Street on the north, Live Oak Street on the south and East Bouldin Creek and the railroad tracks on the east and west. One of the oldest homes connected to the Bouldin family is the L-shaped frame bungalow at **1312 S. First St.**, built about 1894 for Colonel Bouldin's grandson and an excellent example of this once-common design plan.

Nicholas A. Dawson owned a large parcel north of Mary Street and west of South First Street. Between 1890 and 1900, he sold lots in the Dawson Addition and built a number of small houses from locally quarried limestone. Five have been preserved, with one fine example at 1001 W. Mary St. All are four-room bungalows with hexagonal bay windows, an open front porch and double front doors. To make his subdivision more accessible, Dawson built a streetcar line from Barton Springs Road to his higher ground.

Dawson's sister Mary, his construction partner, became principal of South Austin's first public school—the Fulmore School—in 1886, five years after Austin's public school system was organized. The elementary school occupied a white frame one-room schoolhouse at 201 E. Mary St. on the east side of South Congress Avenue. Brackenridge School for "colored" pupils was built nearby. Fulmore has grown into Fulmore Middle School, its alumni including John Henry Faulk and its faculty once including future Texas governor Ann Richards.

North of the Dawson Addition, from South First Street west to the Missouri Pacific Railroad tracks, was a subdivision known for a time as South Heights. Beyond the tracks was a development then known as Evergreen Heights, its borders nearing Kinney Avenue on the west, at South Lamar Boulevard—first named Evergreen Avenue—on the east, Heather Street on the south and just inside Barton Springs Road on the north.

Barton Heights

In far western South Austin, west of South Lamar Boulevard and south of Barton Springs Road, the neighborhood surrounding Kinney Avenue south from Barton Springs Road near Zilker Park filled with small bungalows through the middle decades of the twentieth century. The homes were affordable and convenient, and shopping and businesses were within walking distance. Two-bedroom bungalows in this area can now sell for $500,000, often to be razed and replaced.

Shaded vistas and winding paths in the Umlauf Sculpture Garden are highlighted by the works of noted sculptor Charles Umlauf.

The post–World War II housing boom in South Austin was most evident in Barton Heights and, to the southwest, in Barton Hills, where intensive construction occurred during the '50s. Many of the moderately priced homes along Arthur Lane and Robert E. Lee and Rabb roads were designed and built by architect A. D. Stenger, who did some one hundred homes in the Austin area. Intending "to bring the outside in," Stenger's homes featured rock—often quarried on the site—both inside and out, with low peaked roofs, concrete-tinted floors and low fireplaces. Although his houses lacked central air conditioning, large windows allowed for cross-ventilation. Stenger's "mid-century modern" homes are now targets of preservationists.

One noted resident was sculptor Charles Umlauf, who with his wife, Angie, bought a house and small acreage on a bluff overlooking Barton Springs in 1941. In 1985 Umlauf donated the house, studio and 168 works of sculpture in bronze, alabaster, onyx, polished limestone, primitive stone and wood to the city, which in 1991 built a museum on adjoining property to display the work. The xeriscaped **Umlauf Sculpture Garden** is at 605 Robert E. Lee Rd., at the southern end of Zilker Park.

Parks, Preserves and Greenbelts

Andrew Jackson Zilker arrived in Austin from Indiana in 1876 at the age of 18. He first worked as a dishwasher, then helped build the wooden Congress Avenue bridge. He gradually acquired an ice plant, brickyard, wood and coal business, the electric company and Austin's first Coca-Cola bottling plant. In the early 1900s Zilker, by then known as "the Colonel," began purchasing land along the Colorado River that had belonged to John Rabb and others. In 1917 he donated to the Austin public schools the 35 acres surrounding **Barton Springs,** a popular picnic spot since the 1890s, and gradually donated an adjacent 330 acres to the school system. In 1932 the city, despite the Depression, passed a bond issue to purchase the land from the school system and develop it into Zilker Park.

The Zilker Zephyr winds through much of Zilker Park.

Zilker Metropolitan Park now encompasses the 33-acre **Zilker Botanical Garden** (2220 Barton Springs Rd.); the **Austin Nature and Science Center** on the western edge of the park; the three-acre **Barton Springs Pool,** the only known surface habitat of the lungless Barton Springs Salamander and where Robert Redford learned to swim while his family visited Austin relatives; and a ten-mile system of trails along the **Barton Creek Greenbelt,** which stretches through a gorge to the southwest. A miniature train known as the **Zilker Zephyr** takes passengers through much of the park.

In the parkland stretching east along the south bank of Colorado River–fed Lady Bird Lake, formerly Town Lake, are the **Dougherty Arts Center,** opened in 1947, with an 1,800-square-foot gallery, 150-seat theater and an arts school; the renovated and enlarged **Palmer Auditorium,** a civic center that first opened in 1959; the **Zachary Scott Theatre,** named for the Austin-born movie actor, which began as part of the **Austin Civic Theater** in 1933, relocated in 1972 and now includes the 200-seat **Kleberg Theatre** and the 130-seat Arena Stage;

Austin Lyric Opera studios and the **Long Center for the Performing Arts,** opened in 2008.

Nearby, at South Fifth and Cumberland streets, are the **South Austin Community Gardens,** with 32 plots for organic gardeners.

Other major green spaces are the **West Bouldin Creek Greenbelt** and **Dawson Park** near South First and Gibson streets, the **Blunn Creek Greenbelt** south of Riverside Drive between South Congress Avenue and IH-35, and the **Blunn Creek Preserve** below Oltorf Street and **Gillis Park** near South First and Oltorf streets.

Weird South Austin

We parked on a hilly side street in South Austin one evening to walk a few blocks to the new Long Center for the Performing Arts. The Austin Symphony was playing, and we were season subscribers. The area was an older residential neighborhood near Bouldin Creek with mixed housing stock, ranging from huge limestone piles with verandahs to tiny frame cottages. We had pulled up at the curb near a neatly kept bungalow trimmed in mauve with a large, spherical wooden sculpture painted mauve in the middle of the front lawn.

"Very South Austin," I remarked appreciatively.

My friend Martha sniffed dismissively. She was a longtime resident of Northwest Hills. Unlike Northwest Hills, South Austin, after all, is a place where until recently tie-dye was more common than khaki Bermudas, where the local supermarkets sell Day of the Dead votive candles and post office employees can sport dreadlocks, Afros or beribboned braids.

The sometimes-bizarre dwellings of South Austin were among the Austin phenomena celebrated in the 2005 Dave Steakley play *Keepin' It Weird,* which ran to rave reviews for a couple of months at the Zachary Scott Theatre. These homes tend to be unrestrained by any of the covenants or residents' association rules that fetter upscale suburban developments, and which may limit even the kind of mailboxes owners can install.

For a start, many South Austin homes have multiple add-ons. **Casa Neverlandia,** a 1917 limestone and brick house in the Bouldin Creek neighborhood, had two bedrooms when architect-designer James Talbot bought it for $13,000 in 1979. The house is an environmentally low-impact dwelling, but that isn't all. Talbot and his wife, artist Kay Pils, added extra stories and a tower that have utterly transformed the house. The couple first topped the house with an A-frame that created second and third floors. The four-story lookout tower with views of downtown Austin, elaborate balconies and backyard artist's studio were added later. They used recycled materials salvaged from brick and steelyards, bought from re-use stores or donated by friends.

The house is environmentally low-impact thanks to 16 solar panels on the tower, a rainwater collection system over the studio and gray water from the bath and washer diverted to the garden. There is no central heating or air conditioning, but walls are thick and heavily insulated. In the summer, the owners can sleep outdoors or use a window air conditioner in one room. In the winter, they rely on fireplaces and space heaters. Unique whimsical touches include a speaker tube from the front door to the interior, a pull chime instead of a doorbell and bright, mirrored mosaics and artifacts

A fanciful gable is one of the features added to a 1917 house near Bouldin Creek.

from Mexico, Africa and around the world. Monthly tours of Neverlandia have been available and last about an hour and a half, but must be booked ahead.

Faith Schexnayder runs **Flatfork Studios** and is a fabricator who creates designs in all media, including carved foam and ceramics. She and her husband bought their 1942 three-bedroom Bouldin Creek house in 1992 and have not stopped remodeling. Their home on Gibson Street has a large sculpture of a mother hen prominently nesting in the corner yard. At one point, a vintage pickup sat out front covered with large pieces of fake fruit, part of a Carmen Miranda float used in the First Night Austin 2008 parade.

The **Cathedral of Junk** at 4422 Lareina Drive, beyond Ben White Boulevard in far South Austin, is the creation of Vince Hannemann. In 1989 he lined his fence with hubcaps, then gradually built a tower. Today, the Cathedral is a giant structure you can enter that includes an accretion of bicycles, TVs, metal car parts, toys, utensils and tools that add up to over 60 tons of junk, none of which, he admits, represents any profound philosophical statement.

Hannemann considers himself a "yardist" and also makes collages and sculptures that are for sale. On a framework of many, many lawn mower wheels, car bumpers, kitchen utensils, ladders, cables, bottles, bicycle parts, circuit boards, clocks, illuminated beer signs and other tchotchkes and kitsch, he has built a phenomenon. Called Yardspace 11 because it is his eleventh attempt at such a project, it dwarfs his original 800-square-foot house. At one time Hanneman volunteered at a landfill site for Ecology Action and could scavenge for abandoned items. People continue to bring him stuff—aluminum roosters, for instance. From time to time, he has dismantled and rebuilt the entire structure. In 2000, he tore down a three-story tower in his backyard but couldn't bring himself to get rid of any of the resulting junk.

Newcomers in a nearby townhouse development reportedly have complained to city officials, who occasionally send out inspectors. One such inspector made Hanneman demolish a pile of TVs. The Cathedral has hosted weddings, bachelor parties and CD release parties as well as tour groups of schoolchildren and seniors. It can be visited by appointment only.

Smut Putt Heaven, another once-famous South Austin backyard creation by Scott Stevens, used heads from beauty schools, bottles, plastic lids and cacti to surreal effect. On El Paso Street between South Lamar and South First, a bridge is painted in garishly joyful colors. The **Metropolis Apartments** at 2308 S. Pleasant Valley to the east near E. Riverside Dr. glory in the futuristic murals in vibrant colors painted on its concrete block walls, and are built and operated to eco-friendly standards. The Bouldin Creek neighborhood has a number of 1930s vintage stone cottages with similar whimsical mock-Tudor details.

On Mary Street just west of South Congress, **Nik** the goat grazes happily in a front yard since, despite proven violation of an esoteric livestock code, Mayor Will Wynn granted its owner a special pardon in 2005. A beautifully preserved 1895 house at the corner of Mary and Newton streets features a large pig in its spacious backyard. A sign on the gate informs passers-by that its name is **Starr** and asks them to please refrain from feeding the animal.

SCOPING FOOD FROM CHINA PLATES TO THE SOUP PEDDLER

What helps make dining in South Austin a unique experience is that most of its remarkably varied restaurants are individually owned, not franchises or chains. There is a cornucopia of settings, from outdoor tables beside street vendors to elegant dining rooms in historic homes. Chefs and owners are not afraid to innovate and do not suffer the constraints on originality imposed by a corporate structure.

Mexican and Tex-Mex food has characterized a large number of Austin's best restaurants for decades. A distinctively Austin dish served everywhere is migas, literally translated as "crumbs," made from eggs scrambled with salsa, crumbled corn tortilla chips, cheese and maybe the Mexican sausage chorizo.

These settings can provide some amusing cross-cultural snapshots like the one I got once as a fast food restaurant worker called from behind the counter, "More yellow, Luis! More yellow!" I couldn't understand what the young Anglo guy wanted. More yellow what?

It turned out he needed more ice. He was trying to tell his Spanish-speaking co-worker to bring him some but couldn't convincingly pronounce "hielo," Spanish for "ice." Mystery solved.

I've placed stars (*) next to my special favorites, and you'll no doubt wish to add your own stars to others.

The Dining Legacy of South Austin

Green Pastures * is a rambling house at 811 W. Live Oak St. (441-0215) between South Lamar and South Congress. It was built in 1894 by Dr. E. W. Herndon, a doctor, lawyer and editor originally from Missouri. At the time, Austin's population was only 25,000, and South Austin was almost country. Green Pastures comprised twenty-three acres and bordered on woodland,

Green Pastures, built in 1894 and later home of the family of the noted John Henry Faulk, has been a landmark restaurant since 1946.

with Golden Creek running behind the property. The house had twelve-foot ceilings, generous verandahs, and outbuildings including a kitchen, carriage house and barn. It also had sixteen chicken runs, part of Herndon's Cedar Ranch chicken business. In 1916 attorney Harry Faulk and his wife Mattie Miner Faulk bought the place. Over the years, they raised a large family on the premises. The surrounding area was not fashionable, with transients living in shacks and even in tents down in the creekbed. The Faulks, who kept 35 cows, regularly gave the squatters milk.

There were five Faulk children: Hamilton, Martha, Texana, John Henry and Mary. Hamilton went into the antiques business, Martha worked in education and Texana was involved in education for the deaf. John Henry became a noted CBS radio broadcaster in the 1940s and '50s. Elected vice-president of the American Federation of Television and Radio Artists, he challenged the blacklisting of suspected communists and undesirables during the McCarthy era. As a result, he, too was blacklisted, and he lost his work in radio and television.

After a six-year fight, John Henry won a lawsuit in 1961 with the help of prominent attorney Louis Nizer against an organization that investigated individuals for signs of Communist "disloyalty." The result was a large libel judgment, though Faulk was never able to fully collect the damages. His book Fear on Trial relates these experiences. Faulk later appeared in television and movie roles, traveled on the lecture circuit and toured in his one-man show Pear Orchard, Texas. He died in Austin in 1990 at the age of 76. The city's central public library is named after him.

Judge Faulk's daughter Mary and her husband Chester Koock bought Green Pastures from Mattie Faulk in 1946 and opened a restaurant. The family lived upstairs and ran the restaurant and catering business downstairs. Green Pastures was the first upscale restaurant in Austin to hire an African-American maître d' and staff, serving customers of all races some eighteen years before Austin restaurants were desegregated by law. The Koocks also catered parties at Lyndon Johnson's LBJ Ranch and other events for numerous politicians and celebrities. Having raised seven children, run the restaurant and written several cookbooks and befriended countless people, in the 1950s Mary Faulk Koock was honored as "First Lady of South Austin."

After being damaged in a 1965 fire, the restaurant was refurbished and expanded, though it was never lived in as a home again. The Koocks' eldest son Ken took over the business in 1970 with business partner Lee Buslett. Today peacocks strut beneath the old oak trees on its shaded lawns. Timeless and elegant Green Pastures is famous for its Sunday brunches. It is also a popular spot for dinner, wedding receptions and parties.

Threadgill's World Headquarters at 301 W. Riverside Dr. (472-9304) is another South Austin dining institution with a historic legacy, in this case of Austin music lover and bootlegger Kenneth Threadgill. In 1933 he opened a Gulf filling station just north of the city limits and became the first person in Travis County to acquire a beer and wine license after Prohibition ended. A favorite for traveling musicians with its 24-hour jamming and gambling, it flourished into the 1960s when sometime University of Texas student Janis Joplin sang country and blues there. Kenneth Threadgill closed up shop in 1974 after his wife's death, and Eddie Wilson, creator of the Armadillo World Headquarters, bought the property.

When the Armadillo closed in 1980, Wilson reopened Threadgill's in North Austin; five years later opened a second restaurant, Threadgill's World Headquarters, near the site of the old Armadillo. The South Austin Threadgill's has a '70s memorabilia theme and an outdoor beer garden with live music and features southern cooking. Its specialties include garlic cheese grits, chicken-fried steak and meatloaf. Says Wilson: "In matters of music and food, we represent a time before disco or microwaves."

Two noted establishments started on South Congress Avenue but are no longer there. In 1932 Harry Akin opened the first Night Hawk restaurant on South Congress at Riverside. It became a landmark and a favorite haunt of state politicians. In 1958 Akin began allowing African Americans to dine, making him one of the first local restaurateurs to do so. (On becoming mayor of Austin in 1967, Akin would enforce the then-new civil rights laws.) The Night Hawk chain eventually expanded to seven locations and a frozen-food line. A 1985 fire destroyed the original Night Hawk; although rebuilt, it never regained its clientele and closed in 1989.

Schlotzsky's

In 1971 Schlotzky's opened its first sandwich shop at 1301 S. Congress Ave. and grew from there into a worldwide chain.

In 1971 the first Schlotzsky's sandwich shop opened at 1301 S. Congress Ave., and within a few years it was expanding into the chain that now extends into 35 states and six foreign countries. Though its original location eventually closed, Schlotzsky's lead menu item is still the combination meat, cheese and marinated black olive sandwich developed on South Congress Avenue.

South Congress Avenue

Dominican Joe, 515 S. Congress Ave. (448-3919) at the corner of Riverside Drive, is one of the newest coffee houses in South Austin, and has a secluded courtyard.

Doc's Motorworks Bar and Grill, at 1123 (448-9181), has 31 beers on tap; several flat screens turn this venue into a sports bar on game days.

Jo's Hot Coffee and Good Food * at 1300 (444-3800) next to Hotel San José, is great for people-watching, coffee and pastries. It has the best fried pies in town. It frequently hosts outdoor movies and live music and also provides valet bicycle parking on the first Thursday of each month, when South Congress businesses stay open late and offer sidewalk specials.

For quick meals, **Zen Japanese Food Fast** at 1303 (444-8081) has an extensive Asian menu.

Botticelli, at 1321 (916-1315), has a Mediterranean theme.

For exquisite Italian dining, the handmade artisan food at **Vespaio** *, 1610 (441-6100) makes it the place to go. Opened by chef/owner Alan Lazarus in the late '90s, Vespaio's old storefront setting features exposed brick and glass. Its nightly specials include crispy calamari, spaghetti carbonara and butternut squash-filled ravioli. In 2005, the restaurant expanded next door to open **Enoteca Vespaio** *, a bistro-café that offers antipasti, salads, panini, wood-fired pizzas, pasta and pastries. It also sells gourmet cheeses, deli meats, pâtés, pasta, sauces, olive oils, vinegars, olives, anchovies and imported specialties.

Güero's Taco Bar *, at 1412 (707-8232), opened at its current location in 1994 at Congress Avenue and Elizabeth Street in the hundred-year-old former Central Feed and Seed Building owned by J. M. Crawford. (It was originally located nearby on East Oltorf Street,in the space now housing Curra's.) With its walls covered in photographs of the 1910–20 Mexican Revolution, its nightly specials, live music and much more, Güero's (pronounced "WHERE-ohs") is a busy spot. Its signature dishes include caldo de pollo, a traditional chicken soup with fresh vegetables known for its restorative qualities, and tacos al pastor, rotisserie pork on a corn tortilla with chopped onions, cilantro and pineapple.

Home Slice Pizza * at 1415 (444-7437) serves what some consider the best pizza in South Austin. A to-go window opens to the sidewalk.

The South Congress Café at 1600 (447-3905) features blue corn crepes, beef Milanesa, venison meat loaf and Cajun scampi.

The Woodland at 1716 (441-6800) is great for sandwiches, burgers and salads.

Texas French Bread at 1722 (440-1122) features freshly-baked artisan breads and pastries, along with homemade sandwiches, soups, salads and box lunches.

Fran's Hamburgers at 1822 (444-5738) is one of several locally owned eateries under the same name, this one located here since 1973.

A true Austin institution, the **Magnolia Café** at 1920 (445-0000), has served Southern fare, natural foods and vegetarian dishes for years. A retro-design neon sign says, "Sorry, we're open." Actually open "24 hours, 8 days a week," the Magnolia offers a 24-hour breakfast, soups, salads, sandwiches, burgers, quesadillas and desserts. This is the Magnolia's second location. The first Magnolia, originally called the Omelettry West, was a companion to the Omelettry on Burnet Road but changed its name to Magnolia when it opened on Lake Austin Boulevard.

Nueva Onda, family owned and operated and noted for its Mexican food, is just off the 2000 block of South Congress and a block north of Oltorf at 2218 College Ave. (447-5063).

At 2728, **Habana SoCo** (443-4253) specializes in Cuban dishes like ropa vieja and delicious Cuban sandwiches, though the main La Habana is now downtown.

El Gallo at 2910 (444-6696) is a favorite Mexican and Tex-Mex restaurant. Founded by Abraham Kennedy, who emigrated from Mexico in 1948, in a bungalow on South Congress in 1957, he built the current location in 1968. Kennedy retired in 1980 but came back to work five years later. Today El Gallo serves its third generation of loyal customers, many of whose families have been patrons since the restaurant first opened.

Ruta Maya is a community-oriented coffee house at 3601 (707-9637) near St. Edward's University. It offers fair trade coffee, free Wi-Fi and live music daily and hosts meetings, poetry slams, salsa classes, films and many other events. Its menu includes falafel, tamales and sandwiches.

El Borrego de Oro at 3900 (383-0031) is another favorite Mexican and Tex-Mex restaurant.

On far South Congress beyond Ben White Boulevard, the landmark **Hill's Café** at 4700 (851-9300), started in 1941, when the Goodnight family opened a 20-seat coffee shop next to their motel. Family members were descendants of Texas pioneer Charlie Goodnight, who among much else reputedly invented the chuckwagon. The family's business partner was Sam Hill, hence the café's name. In 1957, the Goodnights bought out Hill but kept the name, by then well-known. Local radio personality Bob Cole took over Hill's in the mid-'90s. It now can hold 500 customers, features live music and flourishes as an authentic Texas Bar-B-Q and steakhouse.

South First Street

South First Street is lined with Mexican restaurants along what has come to be known as the Mexican Mile. They include **El Mercado** at 1302 (447-7445), **Freddie's Place** at 1703 (445-9197), **La Reyna Mexican Restaurant** at 1816 (447-1280), **Polvo's Mexicana and Bar** at 2004 (441-5446), **Little Mexico** at 2304 (462-2188) and **Taquería Arandas** at 2448 (707-0887).

Don't forget **La Mexicana** bakery at 1924 (443-6369), where you can buy authentic flan.

Bouldin Creek Coffee House at 1501 (416-1601) is strictly vegetarian. Dogs on leashes are welcome, and there are bowls of water to prove it.

Jovita's at 1619 (447-7825), which opened in 1992, has three separate dining rooms, a dance floor and a full bar. Striking murals illustrating the history of Texas' indigenous people adorn its walls. Outdoors there's a patio, stage and scenic walkway along Bouldin Creek. Besides great Mexican food, Jovita's live country, folk, bluegrass and rockabilly music draws nightly crowds.

Fair Bean Coffee at 2210 (444-2326) displays sacks of green and roasted coffee and has a calm ambience. It offers five varieties of coffee: Ethiopian, Costa Rican, Honduran, Guatemalan and espresso. Owner Andres Salvador is Venezuelan and serves traditional pastries called rotos filled with cheese, raisins, onions and chicken, as well as empanadas, authentic Spanish omelets and espresso tres leches cake.

For fast food, **Baby Greens** at 2316 (462-1697), just northwest of the burgeoning intersection with Oltorf Street, is a drive-through vegetarian place with healthy natural fast foods, mainly salads, lettuce wraps and tortillas.

Southwest of the intersection, the **Buenos Aires Café** * at 2414 (441-9000) serves breakfast, lunch and dinner featuring traditional Argentinean favorites like pastel de papas (shepherd's pie) and roast chicken.

Baby Greens offers drive-through vegetarian fare.

Summer Moon Coffee Bar at 3115 (804-1665), one block north of Lightsey, serves coffees, teas, empanadas, soups and pastries but is best known for its wood-fired coffee. Summer Moon is just one of several businesses rejuvenating a formerly rather rundown area.

South Lamar Boulevard

Paggi House (473-3700) is at 200 Lee Barton Dr., which parallels to the east the first block of South Lamar Boulevard just below Riverside Drive. It has reopened for dinner only after closing for two years due to the construction of the Bridges on the Park condominiums. Great efforts were made to incorporate the restaurant into the condo site plan; a path connects the patio to the condos. Paggi House boasts a new chef and a new menu.

West of South Lamar and also just below Riverside, at 1701 Toomey Rd., is **Casa de Luz** * (476-2535), Austin's only organic, vegan, macrobiotic restaurant. It's on the campus of the Center for Integral Studies, and proves that healthy food can actually be quite good.

P. Terry's Burger Stand offers pick-ups to eat there or to go.

P. Terry's Burger Stand * at 404 (473-2217), on the corner of Barton Springs Road, is a drive-through that sells delicious beef, chicken and veggie burgers. There are outdoor tables for dining on-site.

Uchi * at 801 (916-4808) serves Japanese fare prepared under the careful eye of executive chef and sushi master Tyson Cole.

Suzi's China Kitchen at 1152 (441-8400) features dine-in or takeout Chinese lunches and dinners.

Maudie's Too, which terms itself "Tex-Mex Heaven," is at 1212 (440-8088). La Feria at 2010 (326-8301), highlights its Mexican offerings with margaritas and mariachi music early Thursday evenings.

Sazón at 1816 (326-4395) features gourmet Mexican food.

Artz Rib House * at 2330 (442-8283) was started by Art Blondin in a caboose just north of the river, but he moved south when he began winning awards for his ribs. Renowned for baby back ribs, brisket, smoked sausage and chicken, Artz has an atmosphere that is pure down home, laid-back, funky South Austin, with red-and-white checked tablecloths and rare "Louisiana Hayride" posters. Blondin is also a musician who has played bass for over 20 years with Jon Emory. There's a bluegrass jam every Sunday afternoon and live music most nights.

In 1997 Argentinean Maria Corbalán started a taco stand in a trailer on a leased site at 2529 (444-0261) that became known as **Maria's Taco Xpress** *. Soon after 2000, the site was sold for a Walgreen's. Developer David Darr also wanted to build a multistory residential building on the property. In a true tale of cooperative collaboration, Darr and Walgreen's worked with Corbalán to develop a permanent taqueria restaurant that is triple the size of the old one. It took three years, but Corbalán was able to buy the acre on which Maria's Taco Xpress now stands. She comments ruefully, "I tried to make it trashy like the old one."

Maria's Taco Xpress is famous for its Sunday brunches with live music, from old-time gospel (earning it the title of "the hippie church") to rock and reggae. It has a full bar and its large patio stage hosts music several nights a week. In 2005 vandals removed the outspread arms from the giant statue of Loca Maria atop the store. Bandages painted with fake blood were subsequently affixed to the stumps to add to the drama, and loyal patrons went into mourning.

Matthew Martinez's **Matt's El Rancho** * (462-9333), now in sprawling new quarters at 2613 (462-9337), has been family owned and operated and serving Mexican cuisine since 1952.

Kerbey Lane Café opened the second of its four Austin restaurants at 2700 (445-4451) in 1986. With a 1950s diner motif, Kerbey Lane is famous for its gingerbread pancakes, omelets, migas and brunch specialties.

One excellent fast food option is the **Rockin' Tomato Pizza Company** at 3003 (447-3351).

At the **Broken Spoke** * dance hall at 3201 (442-6189), (see the Music Scene chapter) patrons tend to like their Lone Star Beer cold and their chicken-fried steaks hot. Their arteries may go into spasm, but it's worth the dining experience now and then.

Its original location on South Congress may be history, but **Schlotzsky's Deli** maintains a South Austin presence just south of the Lamar Street bridge on the west side of the street at 218.

Barton Springs Road

Sandy's Hamburgers at 603 Barton Springs Rd. (478-6322) has held down the corner with South First Street since Andy and Julia Harris opened it in 1946 and named it for their daughter Sandy. A classic drive-through that sells cheeseburgers, hot dogs and root beer, as well as its famous custard, Sandy's is still a bargain. A corn dog is only $1.50, large shakes are $3.02 and on Thursdays and Saturdays a burger, fries and a drink will set you back only $4.10.

The iconic **Shady Grove** restaurant, opened in 1992 at 1624 (474-9991). You'll recognize it by its rustic split-rail fence and wagon wheels and its large, stone-flagged outdoor patio, built in a style developed by Texas State Parks in the '40s. There's also a jukebox and a Hippie Trailer where you can sit while waiting for a table. The eclectic menu runs from cheese fries to margaritas and includes such favorites as its vegetarian Hippie Sandwich and its Airstream Chili. During the warm months, which is about half the year in Austin, it hosts Unplugged at the Grove, an acoustic concert series on Thursday evenings on its outdoor stage. The Starlight Theater also occasionally shows Hitchcock films, westerns, sci-fi and classic movies on the patio.

Just west are the touristy student haunts of **Baby Acapulco** at 1628 (474-8774) and Chuy's, at 1728 (474-4452). Chuy's opened in 1982 and made the media early in the millenium when the Bush daughters were busted for underage drinking there. East of Shady Grove is **Austin Java,** at 1608 (482-9450).

Under pecans shading the patio and deck of **Uncle Billy's Brew-&-Que** at 1530 (476-0100) you can enjoy barbecue and any of the six types of beer Brian Peters brews on site.

Farther east are **Romeo's** at 1500 (476-1090), the **Green Mesquite BBQ** at 1400 (479-0485), and more. Romeo's is the perfect Italian restaurant, family-friendly but also great for date nights and birthday celebrations. The Green Mesquite survived a nearly fatal fire in the '90s and bounced back better than ever.

Uncle Billy's Brew-&-Que brewpub features barbecue and six labels of beer brewed on site.

Vinny's at 1003 (482-8484), a block east of Lamar, is famed for its Italian food.

Oltorf Street

Java Noodles * at 2400 E. Oltorf St. (443-5282) is one of the street's more exotic restaurants, serving wonderful Indonesian and Malaysian food, some of it vegetarian. The ambience is peaceful, and the menu includes coconut curry soup, stir-fry, peanut sauce and banana egg rolls, as well as a Sunday brunch buffet.

You can get light meals and snacks at the bakery and coffee house at **Ventana del Soul,** a community center at 1834 East (707-7447.

Curra's Grill * at 614 East (444-0012) is known for its Mexican specialties.

There's good value at **Habanero Mexican Café** at 501 West (416-0443).

Portable Food

Vaquero Cocina features a full menu, all items prepared streetside in an Airstream trailer.

Lest we forget, portable food in South Austin has proliferated recently. Carts selling breakfast tacos pop up wherever there is a construction site—and there are many these days. Spaces for mobile kitchens usually rent for between $500 and $1,000 a month, depending on the location and size of the site.

A number of crushed ice, Sno-Cone, crepe and tamale vendors operate out of trucks and trailers. **Molly's Sno-Cones** does a brisk summer business on Butler Street near Toomey and South Lamar.

Fliphappy Crêpes * operates from an Airstream trailer in a lot at 400 Jessie St., just west of South Lamar. Fliphappy, which started in 2006, was featured in a Food Network "Throwdown" episode with Bobby Flay in August 2007. Business has flourished since. Included among its offerings are the $6 Cubano crepe with shredded pork, cheddar, Tabasco, pickles and onions.

The Little Sub Trailer can be found at 923 Barton Springs Rd. between Dawson and Bouldin Street in the parking lot of the Austin TriCyclist. It sells such items as cranberry chicken salad sandwiches and tomato basil soup.

Giovanni's Pizza Stand (656-7033), parked in a Mobil gas station lot on South Lamar near Barton Skyway across from Half-Price Books, offers some of the best pizza in town.

Vietnamese sandwiches are the specialty of **Lulu B's** from its site on a lot at 2113 S. Lamar Blvd. near Oltorf (921-4828).

Taste No Evil Muffins at 2531 S. Lamar Blvd. sells from a renovated Austin Dillo trolley in front of Maria's Taco Xpress.

Chris' Little Chicago, 3600 S. Lamar Blvd., is an Italian food-to-go vendor.

A model of a frosted cupcake promotes the wares of Hey, Cupcake!

In a prime location on South Congress, **Hey, Cupcake!** sells delicious and decadent varieties of cupcake from an Airstream in the 1600 block, in a row of trailers that also hosts, among others, **Cornucopia Popcorn, Vaquero Cocina** and **Armadillo Coffee and Tea Company.**

The South Austin Trailer Park and Eatery at 1311 S. First St. has picnic tables and a covered pavilion in a park setting. Here you'll find **Torchy's Tacos**—"gourmet food on a taco"—(366-0537) and **Shuggie's Burgers and Seafood** (789-2063).

The Soup Peddler *, 503 W. Mary St. (373-7672), a.k.a. David Ansel, arrived in Austin from Baltimore in 1998 but soon left his computer programmer job, traveled in Mexico and returned to open a business. In 2002 an e-mail to ten friends with an offer to deliver soup by bike on Sunday mornings launched what has become one of the most remarkable South Austin businesses.

The Soup Peddler sells 700 bowls of soup each week and has some 2,000 regular customers who call themselves "Soupies." Now, however, refrigerated trucks make the deliveries. Ansel's one-story building is painted mustard yellow, as are his trucks, and a "Soup Is Love" sign decorates a window. Besides operating his catering company, Ansel has expanded into entrees and desserts and also feeds the homeless. He has published a best-selling cookbook, *The Soup Peddler's Slow and Difficult Soups: Recipes and Reveries.*

4

SHOPPING FROM SOCO TO SOLA

If you're unfortunate enough not to be living or dining in South Austin, there are still plenty of reasons to stop in and shop. Businesses are diverse, from iconic institutions to the latest word in cool chic. Each of South Austin's major north-south business thoroughfares has its own retail character.

South Congress Avenue

South Congress Avenue—"SoCo"—has an amazing variety of shops and is the most Yuppified South Austin street, though a few used car lots still remain.

South Congress remains home to funky shops like **Lucy in Disguise With Diamonds/Electric Ladyland,** a vintage clothing and costume store at 1506 (444-2002). Two stores that merged into one, the business has held down its block on South Congress for a couple of decades. "Lucy" refers to a Border Collie that belonged to one of the owners.

At **Rue's Antiques** and **Uncommon Object**s at 1500 (442-1775) you may find "the thing you didn't know you wanted."

Other vintage stores include **New Bohemia Retro Resale** at 1606 (326-1238), **Feathers Boutique** at 1700 (912-9779)—specializing in 1940s to '80s clothing and accessories—and **Off the Wall** at 1704 (445-4701), focusing on vintage clothing and estate sales. There is a **St. Vincent de Paul Thrift Store** at 1327 (442-5652).

Chic clothing shops include **Creatures Boutique** at 1206 (707-2500), **by george** at 1400 (441-8600), **Maya Star** at 1508 (912-1475) and **Blackmail** at 1202 (326-7670), which sells only items in black. **American Apparel** has a store at 1325 (441-1400). Allen's Boots at 1522 (447-1413) keeps more than 4,000 pairs of boots in stock.

Gift shops with jewelry, retro kitsch or folk art include **Turquoise Door** at 1208 (480-0618) and **Tesoros Trading Company** at 1500 (447-7500),

One vintage shopping landmark on South Congress Avenue is Lucy in Disguise With Diamonds.

A mural featuring the Virgin of Guadalupe adorns the side wall of Tesoros Trading Company.

which has a notice, "No skating in the store," pasted on its door. **Parts and Labor** at 1604 (326-1648) sells items made exclusively in Texas.

Other gift shops along South Congress are **Mi Casa** at 1700 (707-9797), **Prima Dora** at 1912 (447-4736), **Monkey See, Monkey Do!** at 1712 (443-4999) and **Ten Thousand Villages,** a non-profit at 1317 (440-0440) stocking fairly traded gifts from around the world. **Prototype Vintage Designs** at 1700½ (447-7686) features classic retro furniture. **Hill Country Weavers** at 1701 (707-7396) sells gifts and yarn, and offers classes. At 1400 is **Kidgenius Toy**s (448-2200), a hip store for kids

Among galleries are **Avenue Gallery** at 1510 (442-3600),

Austin Art Glass at 1608 (916-4527) and **Gallery SoCo** at 1714 (442-5144). **Yard Dog Folk Art,** next to **Maya Star** in a 1932 building at 1510 (912-1613), specializes in folk art.

The Great Outdoors Nursery and its **Garden District Coffee House** at 2810 (462-2473) is a place to relax and select unique planters and yard art.

Ecowise, just off South Congress at 110 Elizabeth St. (326-4474 or 326-2339), has dozens of energy saving, ecologically safe and aesthetically designed items.

The **Herb Bar** at 200 W. Mary St. (444-6251) has been a neighborhood fixture since 1986. Blossoming in an ivy-shrouded building, it resembles an old apothecary shop, but the interior is light and airy. The Herb Bar sells natural health and bodycare products, handmade cards, candles, beeswax, books and meditation aids and offers alternative health treatments such as massage and neuromuscular energy healing. Owner Twila Willis took over in 1995, and some products are her creations. From the 1900s to the 1930s, the century-old stone building was a general store operated by Robert S. Stanley, one of South Austin's first African-American businessmen.

The Herb Bar has occupied a century-old ivy-shrouded building since 1986.

Grocery stores are **Cissi's Market** at 1400 (225-0521) and the **Farm to Market Grocery** at 1718 (462-7220).

Far to the south is the more conventional H-E-B grocery, at South Congress and Oltorf. It's large and usually crowded, and its patrons and staff probably speak more Spanish than English. You can glimpse a sharply dressed young cashier dude with spiked hair tenderly escorting a bent elderly woman with long white braids to a waiting car. Could be his grandmother. Children clutch balloons as mothers load them into grocery cart seats. Outdoor stands sell menudo and lawn ornaments in the form of the Virgin Mary. Inside, votive candles for every occasion or problem—"Work," "Love," "Luck"—fill an entire aisle. This is not your pastel-toned, subdued H-E-B of far northwest Austin.

Across South Congress Avenue from St. Edward's University, the smallish **South Austin Farmers Market** operates year round on Saturdays from 8 a.m. to 1 p.m. in the **El Gallo Restaurant** parking lot.

On First Thursday each month, merchants hold sidewalk sales with live music, food samples and other events. Shops stay open until 10 p.m. Free Dillo buses have run from One Texas Center at 500 Barton Springs Rd. to South Congress on those evenings, so parking hasn't been an issue, but there are rumors that Capital Metro plans to drastically curtail Dillo routes and start charging fares.

South First Street

South First Street has sidewalks, places to eat, many owner-occupied businesses and a funky neighborhood vibe that may mean it will become South Austin's new main drag, preserving the spirit of the old South Austin.

South First anchors South Austin's oldest Hispanic neighborhood. Evoking this past is **Cantu's Mexican Imports,** a longtime fixture at 1500 (448-2677) that sells dried aromatic herbs, healing ointments, cards, religious items and good luck charms (milagros) as well as imported incense, jewelry, piñatas, serapes, hammocks and sombreros. Cantu's first store opened on West Mary Street in 1983. As curanderos, or healers, the Cantus also do aura readings, health analysis, channeling and energy work. Curanderismo establishes links between spiritual and physical illness and offers cures. It's part of folk healing—if used for evil purposes, called brujería—but for the business's founder the enterprise reflected his charismatic Catholicism.

At **Roadhouse Relics** at 1720 (442-6366), Todd Sanders sells signs, neon and "modern vintage" items from the '50s and '60s. Flashback Vintage Boutique is a venerable vintage clothing shop at 1805 (445-6906).

El Corazon Center at 2209 gathers several unique owner-run businesses in one spot. **End of an Ear** (462-6008) specializes in rare vinyls of indie pop, retro, jazz, soul, European pop, reggae, hip-hop and more. **New Brohemia** (804-0988), a men's vintage clothing store at 2209, is run by the owners of New Bohemia and **Parts and Labor** on South Congress Avenue. happiness (440-8600) offers garden, gifts and home items including plants, art, clothing, jewelry and furniture, many made by local crafts people. **Amelia's Retro-Vogue and Relics** next door at 2213 (442-4446) started in the 1980s on South Congress and moved to South Lamar before settling here.

Unbridaled, a hip bridal shop at 1106 (444-2743), opened in 2004 and is famous for its simple yet classic, sometimes vintage-inspired wedding and bridesmaids' dresses and accessories. Nearby are **Polish Nail Spa** at 1002 (448-1803); **Shag Salon** hair designs at 908 (851-7424); and **Love,** opened in 2002 at 1000 (442-5683) with fashion items as well as furniture and accessories for the home and occasional live music in the form of "Love on the Lawn" concerts.

Secret Oktober, in a distinctively painted blue and black building at 1905 (462-9217), specializes in Goth, punk and alternative clothing. **Pedazo Chunk** at 2009 (441-3505) is an independent video store with an outdoor patio and a screening room. **Greater Austin Garbage Arts** at 2214 is an artists' collective that re-uses building supplies and materials and displays works made from salvaged materials.

Resistencia Bookstore, 1801-A S. First Street (416-8885), moved to South Austin in 1983. The late Raúl Salinas—or "raúlralinas," as he referred to himself—founded the original Resistencia in East Austin in 1981 as a neighborhood center, inspired partly by Seattle's Centro de la Raza. An Austinite who migrated to Seattle and San Francisco, Salinas was a poet and activist. He died in 2007, but his memory and dedication to civil rights live on. Resistencia specializes in Native American, Chicano, Latino, African American, gay, lesbian and children's bilingual literature, welcomes aspiring writers, has meeting space for community organizations and welcomes such groups as the Austin Cuba Committee and the Leonard Peltier Support Group and Pastors and Veterans for Peace, which sends delegations to Cuba and Nicaragua. It also houses Red Salmon Arts, a grassroots Native American/Chicano cultural center working with the indigenous communities of Austin. Red Salmon Press, an editorial collective begun in 1981, has published commercial newsletters and informational leaflets as well as several literary collections.

On a side street, **Café Caffeine** at 909 W. Mary St. (447-9473) once housed "Two Unemployed Democrats," which sold political buttons, T-shirts and paraphernalia.

South Lamar Boulevard

While South Lamar Boulevard—"SoLa"— remains for now the most conventional commercial strip of all three South Austin streets, drowning as it is in used car dealerships, fast food restaurants and copy shops, it has its own claims to fame.

For one, Whole Foods Market, since departed from South Austin, got its start here. In 1978, 25-year-old college dropout John Mackey and his girlfriend borrowed money from family and friends to open a small natural foods store in Austin called SaferWay, its name chosen as a spoof of Safeway. By 1980, the business had merged with Clarksville Natural Foods to become Whole Foods Market. In time, Mackey opened his second store on South Lamar, where it remained for over 15 years.

In 1984 Whole Foods expanded to Houston, Dallas and New Orleans and by 1989 to the West Coast. In 2002 it opened a location in Toronto. Two years later there were stores in Britain. By the next year Whole Foods had built a flagship store and corporate headquarters in Austin just north of the river at Lamar and Sixth Street.

At 1516 S. Lamar Blvd. (443-2292) is one of the city's five **Planet K** shops, which sell smoking accessories and gifts and houses the **South Austin Museum of Popular Culture,** which opened in 2004 with a poster exhibition as part of SXSW. A non-profit, the museum holds eight exhibitions a year and is staffed by part-time volunteers. The gallery features posters by Jim Franklin, and there is an outside wall of memorials to Texas musicians who have passed on, like Tex Ritter and Biscuit Turner. A coffee stand, the **Grateful Shed,** is attached, and a planter in back of the business is made from a junked car.

Just west of South Lamar, at 1501 Barton Springs Rd. and Kinney Avenue, is the home of **Flipnotics Coffeespace** (480-8646), with its clothing and gift shop downstairs and a cool and inviting café with a large, welcoming verandah upstairs. In business here since 1992, Flipnotics has several other spinoffs around Austin with its "cool threads and hot coffee."

Moxie and the Compound (441-MOXY), with locally designed eclectic clothes, accessories and art, is at 2110 South Lamar.

An **Alamo Drafthouse Theater** has a location at 1120 (476-1320). Tim and Karrie League opened the original Alamo Drafthouse downtown in 1997. The drafthouse concept combines dinner and a movie by replacing every other row of seats with tables and offering a varied menu of pizzas, salads, sandwiches, wine and beer. Wait staff in black glide silently between the rows to serve as patrons watch the screen. By 2001, the Leagues had opened a second Alamo Drafthouse and four years later inaugurated the six-screen theater on South Lamar, with an eclectic series of every genre from bizarre and hard-to-find to first-run movies and classics to arcane, exotica and forgotten films. Each September comes Fantastic Fest, with sci-fi, horror, fantasy, cult and Asian films. Regular events are Sing-Alongs, Music Mondays, Terror Tuesdays, Weird Wednesdays and the Austin Air Guitar Competition.

On South Lamar near Oltorf Street, a row of shops past and present selling used furniture, collectibles and antiques has borne names noteworthy in themselves. They've included **Austentatious, Austin Found** and **Bead It,** at 2058 (693-2323), Texas's largest bead store, which also offers classes.

THE SOUTH AUSTIN MUSIC SCENE

Downtown Austin is renowned for the several blocks of Sixth Street east of Congress Avenue that have evolved into a locus of bars and live music venues. Further east across Interstate 35, historically minority East Austin has been known for blues venues, barbecue joints and after-hours clubs.

Neither area can boast the variety and funk of South Austin's music.

South Austin has dozens of venues, from tiny taco restaurants that feature live music one evening a week to the vast outdoor stages of Auditorium Shores. Some date from the Vietnam protest years of the 1960s, when Austin was a destination for hippies from Lubbock or Abilene, a place more liberal than their hometowns, a destination where they could fit in and ultimately "find themselves."

Tiny restaurants are among the dozens of venues featuring live music in South Austin.

South by Southwest, the music, film and media conference–cum–festival better known by its initials, SXSW, would not have been possible without the crucible of the South Austin music scene to inspire it. The event began in 1987 as a battle of the bands north of the Colorado at the Austin Convention Center. Now a multiday extravaganza held each March, it attracts 1,400 performers from throughout the world and is the city's largest money-making public event.

Austin also experienced its share of folk music in those years.

Rod Kennedy started the Zilker Park Folk Festival in 1965 and opened a downtown Austin club called the Chequered Flag in 1966. He later founded the Kerrville Folk Festival.

The South Austin progressive country band Freda and the Firedogs was formed in 1972 featuring Louisiana-influenced Marcia Ball's vocals and piano. The band often played at the Split Rail, a venue on South Lamar Boulevard near Lady Bird Lake that opened in 1962 and flourished until 1978. After performing at a Broken Spoke benefit for Lloyd Doggett's Texas Senate election bid, the Firedogs earned a steady Friday night gig at the Spoke. Wayne Hancock recorded "The South Austin Sessions." One bluegrass band that performs today named itself the South Austin Jug Band.

Four Institutions

The **Continental Club,** at 1315 S. Congress Ave. (441-2444), is a legend in its own right, as many of the big names have played there. The 2,500-square-foot building housed a Laundromat back in 1947, but has become a roots rock haven. Its life as a music venue began in 1955 when Morin Scott opened a swank supper club at this location a few blocks south of the river, then almost the edge of town at a time when South Austin was almost an afterthought for most inhabitants of the capital city.

The Continental Club originally advertised "combo music and charcoal-broiled steaks." Jimmy Dorsey and boyish singing quartets played here.

Originally a BYOB place, it is thought to have been the first establishment in Travis County to sell liquor by the drink. During the 1960s, the venue became a strip club featuring the likes of Candy Barr and Bubbles Cash. Under new ownership in the 1970s, it became a showcase for musicians like bluesman Stevie Ray Vaughan, the Joe Ely Band, the Cobras, Leroy Parnell, W. C. Clark and Charlie and Will Sexton.

The Continental Club has become a South Austin music legend since its opening in 1955.

When Steve Wertheimer bought the club in 1987, he feared that few would venture out at night to hear music on the sketchy thoroughfare South Congress had become. Wertheimer, a University of Texas graduate who grew up in Houston, needn't have worried. By the start of the 21st century, South Congress's junkies, prostitutes and the porn theater were gone, and the gun shop next to the club had closed and been replaced by a boutique clothing store. The revamped Continental Club mixes musicians, newcomers, celebrities, tourists and South Austin Bubbas. Although luminaries such as Quentin Tarantino, Sandra Bullock, Sheryl Crow, Drew Barrymore, Johnny Depp, Jennifer Anniston, Dwight Yoakum, Ray Davies and Benjamin Bratt have visited, their presence has fazed neither staff nor patrons. Wertheimer has opened a larger Continental Club spin-off in Houston.

Another survival of the era is the iconic **Broken Spoke,** established at 3201 South Lamar Boulevard (442-6189) in 1964. James White founded the honky-tonk after a stint in the Army. Pondering what to do with his life, he decided to bank on his love of country music and built the Broken Spoke a mile south of the river in a then semi-rural area. The low frame structure was set well back from the road and sheltered by a large oak tree out front. There had always been beer joints in South Austin and country and western dance halls at the edge of town, but the Spoke was special.

It opened on November 10, 1964, with 300 patrons present. A true Texas dance hall serving food and beer, the Spoke's interior still includes a long, low room with a small stage at one end and a large dance floor. White was soon booking country stars like Bob Wills, Roy Acuff, Hank Thompson, Tex Ritter, the Sons of the Pioneers, Ray Price, Kitty Wells, Grandpa Jones, Willie Nelson, Kris Kristofferson and George Strait. In recent years, performers at the Spoke have included Gary P. Nunn, Sam and Son, The Geezinslaw Brothers, the Derailers, the late Don Walser, Chris Wall and Dale Watson.

Founder White wrote "The Broken Spoke Legend," recorded by Alvin Crowe on his album *Pure Country.* For the Spoke's twenty-fifth anniversary in 1989, White opened the Tourist Trap Room and filled it with memorabilia, hats, photos of country and western performers and other treasures. The Spoke changed owners in 2007 but continues to flourish, drawing crowds that span decades, from the elderly to the young.

The Saxon Pub at 1320 S. Lamar Blvd. (448-2552) continues to be a popular place to hear blues, country and rock. A huge statue in the parking lot decked out in a full suit of armor and nicknamed "Sir Dance-A-Lot" draws

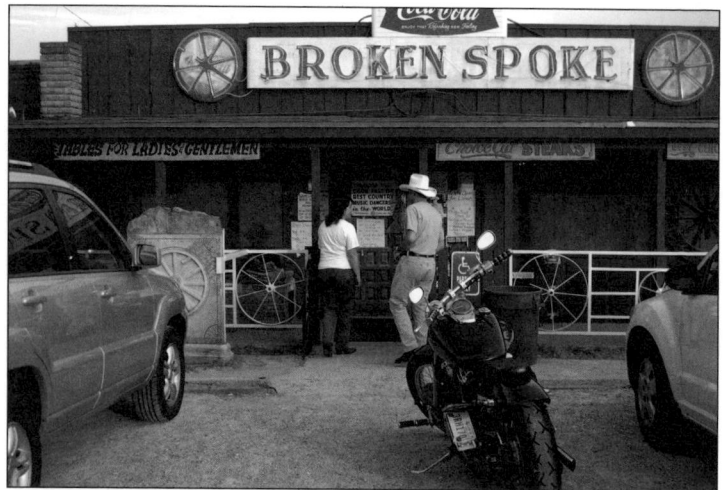

The Broken Spoke, a classic Texas dance hall serving food and beer, opened in 1964.

attention, though the club's strip mall location itself is unprepossessing. Matthew McConaughey is remembered as having danced there with a pool cue.

The Horseshoe Lounge, another South Austin institution, at 2034 S. Lamar Blvd. (442-9111), comes across as the quintessential dive bar, with more credibility. Its padded, horseshoe-shaped bar basically serves beer in cans, cash only. Though it has a pool table, shuffleboard and NASCAR décor, but the Horseshoe's main feature is a jukebox that plays country, album rock and pop music.

Other Good Bets

Jovita's Tex-Mex Restaurant at 1619 S. First St. is a good example. Nightly, except Mondays, it offers music ranging from blues to country, from the hottest local groups to touring bands, in a comfortable, family-oriented atmosphere. Couples spin on the dance floor and parents dance with their kids in a setting intimate enough that the performers become almost family. The Derailers, the Cornell Hurd Band, the Gourds and many others play here regularly. There's a $5 to $7 cover charge weekends.

Ruta Maya, a cavernous coffeehouse and unofficial community activism center at 3601 S. Congress Ave. near St. Edward's University, has live music each Wednesday through Sunday. Tuesday night is open mike with no cover charge. Wednesday is Cuban night, where a $5 cover charge gets you salsa lessons. Other evenings showcase big band, swing, battles of the bands, soca, reggae and reggaeton.

Trophy's Bar & Grill at 2008 S. Congress Ave. is a dive that blasts punk, indie, metal and rock. Tuesdays are reserved for a singer/songwriter showcase of mainly acoustic music, while Wednesday night it's rock'n'roll and Thursday is rockabilly time, often featuring local band Two Hoots and a Holler. Music continues on weekend nights, usually with an $8 cover.

The legendary **Hill's Café,** situated under hundred-year-old oaks at 4700 S. Congress Ave. beyond Ben White Boulevard just outside the informal boundary of South Austin, caters to a different crowd, playing live C&W Tuesday through Sunday. Established and rising country stars Kevin Fowler, Cory Morrow, Charlie Robison, Rick Trevino and Jason Boland and the Stragglers are some of the recent and future performers booked for Hill's outdoor stage. It's said you cannot legitimately consider yourself an Austinite until you've tasted barbecue here. "Better find your way back home to Hill's" runs this establishment's theme song.

Most South Austin restaurants include regular live music. These include **Güero's Taco Bar** at the corner of South Congress Avenue and Elizabeth Street, which has live music Thursday through Sunday 6:30 to 9 p.m. and sometimes on weekend afternoons. The outdoor stage at **Freddie's Place,** 1703 S. First Street, hosts music at 6 p.m. Thursday through Saturday and at various times on Sunday. **The Green Mesquite BBQ** ("Horrifying Vegetarians Since 1988") at 1400 Barton Springs Rd., enjoys open mike on Thursday and live music Friday through Sunday.

It's a good idea to call restaurants first to check out their music schedule. You can also consult their websites or pick up a copy of Austin's alternative weekly, *The Austin Chronicle,* out each Thursday and not only packed with local information but also noted for its investigative reporting.

In Memoriam

In 1969 an Austin hippie rock emporium called the Vulcan Gas Company closed. Located downtown just off Congress Avenue, it was Austin's first real rock music venue when it opened in 1967, booking performers like Muddy Waters, the Velvet Underground and country rock band Poco. Eddie Wilson was then the manager of local rock group Shiva's Headband, whose music ran to twenty-minute psychedelic sets that secured a contract with Capitol Records. Wilson booked the band into honky-tonks like the

Cactus Club in South Austin, but with the demise of the Vulcan he was seeking a new venue.

Wilson soon noticed an abandoned National Guard Armory on Barton Springs Road and envisioned it as a possible performance space. Built in the late 1940s, the building was near a roller-skating rink and had poor acoustics and no air conditioning. But it had 30,000 square feet and could hold 1,500 persons, and it was available at a cheap rent. Local artist Jim Franklin, who frequently used armadillos as a motif, was hired to create advertising posters, and the name Armadillo World Headquarters evolved. Kit Thompson recalls that there was also an Armadillo Racing Club north of the river located at Lavaca and 18th Streets, patronized by racecar enthusiasts. That influenced the choice of name for the Armadillo. Many regulars who raced and worked on cars migrated south of the river to hang out at the Headquarters.

The Headquarters opened on August 7, 1970, with Wilson and partners Bobby Hedderson and Mike Tolleson at the helm. Jan Beeman, an Armadillo cook whose kitchen advertised "Good Food Cheap," was a mother figure to many of the musicians. Genres and generations mixed more freely than on Sixth Street. Almost everyone sat on the semi-carpeted floor—businessmen, hippies and cowboys. The admission fee was minimal, and marijuana was tolerated. The hall was never raided, the story being that the police weren't anxious to arrest local or state politicians or their own officers.

The Armadillo paralleled the Fillmore East in San Francisco and was profiled in *Time* magazine and *Rolling Stone.* Its blend of country and rock became known as "the Austin Sound," "Redneck Rock" and "Cosmic Cowboy" music. Acts included Frank Zappa, ZZ Top, AC/DC, Dire Straits, the Fabulous Thunderbirds (whose Keith Ferguson was once married to Austin blues belter Lou Ann Barton), the Jerry Garcia Band, Levon Helm, Emmylou Harris, Waylon Jennings, Jerry Lee Lewis, Lynyrd Skynyrd, Iggy Pop, Rush, Van Halen, the Ramones, Van Morrison and Bruce Springsteen, who played there often in the '70s. Tickets to hear Ray Charles were $7, though he appeared only by default when his original venue became unavailable. Willie Nelson, a Texan who relocated to Austin from Nashville in 1971, also played at the Armadillo. The hall sometimes booked opera and ballet.

"We were making a living, enjoying what we were doing and could be proud of it," said Eddie Wilson in *Austin: Remember When,* a 1996 documentary that aired on local PBS station KLRU. "There were few places where bands could play original material. We didn't have to wear ties or work for someone else . . . There was a social-cultural-economic boom, and the lifestyle itself was an art form . . . We could take pleasure in it on a daily basis, and call it a job."

Advertisements for 1970s performances at the Armadillo have become collectors' items. Posters designed by Jim Franklin, Danny Garrett, Michael Priest, Guy Juke, Kerry Awn and Pauline Walsh Jacobson can be found at the Center for American History at the University of Texas. Many of the artists were inspired by Seymour Fogel, a noted Texas Modernist abstract muralist from New York who apprenticed with Mexican muralist Diego Rivera, taught at the University of Texas from 1946 to 1959 and lived at 2411 Kinney Ave.in South Austin.

The Armadillo opened a beer garden and started food service in 1972 but always struggled financially. It began to lay off staff in 1976 and filed for Chapter 11 bankruptcy protection the next year. Increasing property taxes caused the owner to raise the rent, and there were many offers to buy the land. The final concert took place on New Year's Eve 1980 and featured Asleep At the Wheel. The Armadillo's contents were sold at auction. It took a whole day to dig up a wisteria tree and move it to someone's South Austin garden. The property was reportedly sold for $4 to $8 million. The building was razed and replaced by an office tower, One Texas Center. In 2006 the City of Austin dedicated a plaque where the Armadillo and its beer garden once stood, declaring it a place where "art, music and the spirit of Austin flourished."

One legacy is the Armadillo Christmas Bazaar, begun in 1976 at the Armadillo World Headquarters and now held annually in the Austin Convention Center. Another is the theme music for Austin City Limits, the KLRU music show inspired by the Armadillo. The program's success resulted in the first Austin City Limits Festival, held since 2002 at Zilker Park and now a three-day event each September that draws 65,000 people to hear 130 bands on several stages. First aired in 1976, the TV show is the longest-running concert program on PBS and a significant factor in Austin's title as "Live Music Capital of the World." The theme includes lines from musician Gary P. Nunn's "London Homesick Blues":

> *I wanna go home with the armadillo,*
> *Good country music from Amarillo and Abilene,*
> *The friendliest people and the prettiest women you've ever seen.*

The Armadillo was geared to major touring acts, but there were other places to hear great live local music in Austin. The Soap Creek Saloon, described as both a honky tonk in the hills and a fantastically decrepit roadhouse, was started by George Majewski on a dirt track off Bee Caves Road in 1973. Just finding it and getting up the road was an achievement that called for a round of Tecates. In 1979 the Saloon relocated to North Lamar for a while before coming to rest on Academy Drive just off South Congress, a stone's throw from the Armadillo and the Continental Club. The Soap Creek Saloon had faded by 1985, but many Austinites have fond memories of the Saloon and its music.

Academy Drive saw the opening of Willie Nelson's Texas Opry House in the early '70s, though it folded in 1974. The venue reopened in 1975 as the Austin Opry House with Willie and Waylon Jennings playing opening night, and was home to many musicians until the '80s when it morphed into a recording venue, Arlyn-Pedernales Studios. Beginning in 1984, Arlyn has recorded artists such as Bonnie Raitt, Kris Kristofferson, Neil Young and Lucinda Williams. The building later housed the local chapter of the American Federation of Musicians, the Austin Guitar School, a management company and an independent record label.

EVENTS FOR ALL SEASONS

South Austin likes to make bold statements. It doesn't do things by halves. Sedate garden parties, solemn ceremonies and timid gatherings are simply not its style. Whenever there's a South Austin event, you'll hear about it before, during and after it happens.

Bat Fests and Kite Fests

An event on South Austin's northern border that draws national attention is the annual **Bat Fest,** held each August. A colony of Mexican free-tailed bats began forming in 1980 under the South Congress Avenue bridge and now numbers 1.5 million, making it the largest urban bat colony in North America. They gather each March and April and in October return to Mexico for the winter, having set out each summer evening at dusk to devour up to 30,000 pounds of insects. You can watch from the bridge or from boats.

Zilker Park, on the western edge of South Austin, draws over 25,000 people every March to the annual **Zilker Park Kite Festival,** held since 1929. For many years the park has been the site of the **Trail of Lights,** held for ten days before Christmas, when corporate sponsors outdo each other in staging brilliantly lit seasonal displays with animation and music. Summers at the Hillside Theater feature **Shakespeare in the Park** and the **Zilker Summer Musical. Blues on the Green,** on Wednesday evenings throughout the summer, showcases top musicians. **The Zilker Park Fall Jazz Fest, Zilker Gardens Fest** and **Fourth of July Concert** featuring the Austin Symphony Orchestra, plus numerous other events, round out the year.

Soccer clubs practice and play in the park; joggers and walkers enjoy the hike-and-bike trail; and the Zilker Zephyr, a miniature train, departs from a station near the children's playground.

The Zilker Park Kite Festival has been held in March since 1929.

Farther east along Barton Springs Road, the Palmer Events Center hosts the **Citywide Garage Sale** several times a year, drawing buyers and sellers of everything from Depression glass to advertising memorabilia and vintage clothing.

Beginning in 2005, **Art Outside** occurred on two weekends every March or April in an oddly shaped three-acre area off West Oltorf near South Lamar called the Enchanted Forest, a former hobo encampment. Some 200 artists showed their work as live music played. The site also hosted occasional fund-raisers for non-profit groups. Albert DeLoach bought the property in 1997, combining three lots and living with his family on one while allowing artists to use the other two for large installations. His goal was to create a self-sustaining arts and community center, and he maintains that at least 150 artists used the space in 2008. Permanent art such as a giant rocking horse and a 16-foot-high sculpture made of bottles, brass and old lamps eventually appeared along the trails. Over the years multiple stages, electricity and fire pits became part of the site.

In July 2008, however, the city withdrew DeLoach's temporary use permit for the site, citing problems including temporary structures built without permits, electrical code violations and occasional noise issues. Officials told

DeLoach he must file a plan with the city to obtain a conditional use permit. DeLoach had built a giant heart from refrigerator parts on his property, and he began enclosing the heart with a bamboo fence as a symbolic protection against the city's onslaught. He had to cancel performances by two theater companies, as well as a fund-raiser for several local co-ops, and there were fears that he might have to cancel his annual **Haunted Forest Trail,** a Halloween event that raises money for Art Outside.

The **Austin Art Car Parade** occurs every fall, when fabulously decorated vehicles roll down Congress Avenue to convene in a South Congress parking lot. The annual **Lonestar Rod and Kustom Round-Up,** founded in 2004 by Steve Wertheimer and others, takes place each April at the Travis County Expo Center and at locations along South Congress Avenue. **The Keep Austin Weird Festival** and **5-K Run** was launched in 2003 and includes concerts at Auditorium Shores. In 1994 a bronze-dipped statue of the late blues guitarist Stevie Ray Vaughan, in trademark cape and flat-brimmed hat, was placed near the riverbank at Auditorium Shores, just west of a gazebo and the First Street Bridge. Vaughan perished in a helicopter crash in 1990. Visitors often leave flowers and notes at the statue, especially on October 4, Vaughan's birthday.

Remembering Aqua Fests and Billion Bubba Marches

South Austin has drawn its share of crowds to weird and wonderful happenings that have since ended. In 1962, the Chamber of Commerce created the Austin Aqua Fest to promote the city and nearby Highland Lakes as a tourist destination. The first Aqua Fest, a 10-day August event, featured speedboat races and music, with Art Linkletter of "People Are Funny" fame appearing as headliner. In 1980 the AquaFest moved from the north side of Lady Bird Lake to the south side's Auditorium Shores. Radio stations and corporate sponsors promoted the Fest and helped book nationally known acts like Linda Ronstadt on multiple stages.

As attendance reached 252,000 by 1985, nearby Bouldin Creek neighborhood residents complained about noise and traffic congestion. The city moved some activities to a lake near Austin but also began to withdraw financing. While the Fest remained based at Auditorium Shores, it downsized and became more of a music event than a civic event. Dolly Parton was the main attraction in 1992, but by then ticket prices had gone up and attendance was down to 44,000. The next year there was a loss of over $700,000. The event began booking mostly local bands, relied on an all-volunteer staff, returned to theme nights featuring country and western or Mexican music and finally held the last Aqua Fest in 1998. Ongoing Auditorium Shores music events include **Reggae Fest** each April.

Then there was the Tug of Honor. From 1987 to 1989, Yuppies vied with Bubbas in a tug of war across the Colorado River, pulling on a rope strung across a 300-foot-wide stretch of Lady Bird Lake. Just picking up the thing was considered heroic. The tug-of-war was the brainchild of former state Rep. Charles Gandy to raise funds for the Austin Youth Hostel. Hundreds of onlookers lined both sides of the river, eating, drinking and cheering on the contestants. Beer and barbecue were served on the south side, wine and quiche on the north. It is unclear why the Tug of Honor ended after three years, but it may have been because the South Austin team tended to win.

On October 14, 2000, the Billion Bubba March in South Austin drew several hundred residents, politicians and musicians. They marched three blocks south from a Wells Fargo Bank parking lot to the Broken Spoke to advocate for voter registration, call humorous attention to community improvement, honor diversity and keep in touch with what makes South Austin unique. The march was planned by former Bouldin Creek Neighborhood Association president Jack Speer and his wife, Carol Kallendorf, following the inspiration of the South Austin Culture Club, founded by Jack Speer and others to promote and preserve the uniqueness of South Austin while calling attention to serious issues. Said organizer Speer: "South Austin has more culture in a sixteen-mile swath than in all America." One politician quipped, "It's not about leaving your pickup truck up on blocks in your front yard. We're beyond that. It's about helping your brother-in-law get his pickup down off the blocks and getting it running again—even if you don't like your brother-in-law."

John Kelso, satiric *American-Statesman* columnist and longtime South Austin resident, was grand marshal and emcee. Musicians included Ponty Bone and the Squeezetones, Gina Lee and Her Texas Three, Los Pinkys, Blue Diamond Shine, On the Air and the tie-dyed South Austin Gospel Choir. Gary Hyatt, later the Bouldin Creek Neighborhood president, received a plaque—designed on a hubcap from the vast collection of eccentric South Austin resident Hubcap Annie—for registering the most new voters of any neighborhood.

Other Culture Club inspirations include the Green Pastures Cornflab, the Whole Enchilada, Penn Field–Too Cool to Bulldoze, Town Lake Park Openings I and II and South Austin Jeopardy.

LIFE IN THE RV PARKS

One of South Austin's most striking features is a prime section of Barton Springs Road that became home to three trailer parks—and is still home to two. Shady Grove RV Park centered the trio, with Mobile Manor to the west and Pecan Grove RV Park to the east. They were within the three-block stretch of Restaurant Row that includes Shady Grove Restaurant, the rambling burger joint with outdoor seating, and long-time favorites like Chuy's, Baby Acapulco and the Green Mesquite B-B-Q.

Havens of leafy quietude most of the year, livened by exuberant squirrels, the trailer parks are gloriously lush and green in summer. Despite their proximity to a busy thoroughfare, the sounds of rumbling trucks and wailing sirens seem far away. Occupants do not own their sites, and nearly all the parks' spaces are rented on a month-to-month basis, but many residents live there as long as ten—and even twenty—years. There are long waiting lists.

Most residents occupy their sites full time. A few are kept open for short-term visitors. Rents range from $350 to $450 and include utilities. A bank of mailboxes, a laundry room, showers and a few shelves of books that pass for a lending library in the office are the main amenities. Dwellers, a mix of retirees, students, professionals, artists and musicians, live in an almost urban village atmosphere. You can get to know your neighbors easily, or you can enjoy as much privacy as you like. Residents are concerned with one another's health, welfare and happiness, and there is a strong feeling of solidarity.

Shady Grove, established in the 1940s, was the first such park in South Austin. Former park owner Susan Toomey Frost remembers that her father bought the land in 1922 when South Austin was semirural, intending to plant trees and develop a working pecan grove. But the pecan industry faced tough competition from Georgia pecans, and the business did not flourish.

In the late 1940s when motor tourism spawned trailers and motels, Toomey Frost's uncle Dan Toomey started pouring concrete slabs. A trailer park with some thirty sites emerged among the remaining pecans. Dan Toomey continued to live there well into his 90s. Several occupants were nurses, which eased concerns over his increasing frailty. Shady Grove is now history, sold to developers in 2007 for upscale condominiums. The displaced tenants included new Austin Police Chief Art Acevedo, who lived there for some months while house hunting after moving to Austin. A restaurant of the same name still stands on the site.

Just west of the late Shady Grove is Mobile Manor, a tidier and more suburban spot than the two older parks that still shares the same convenient location near Zilker Park.

Fifteen Years in Pecan Grove

Pecan Grove RV Park, an Austin institution since 1946, opened as the Austin Trailer Mart. Its 94 sites make it the largest of the original trio, and home to over 130 residents. Though surrounded by traffic congestion and the cacophony of rampant construction, most recently for adjacent condominiums, its long avenues of old oak and pecan trees provide a shady canopy most of the year, though the park can appear a bit barren on a rainy winter day.

My husband was living at the Pecan Grove RV Park when we met. He had lived abroad for 16 years. On returning to America, he bought a truck and a fifth-wheel trailer to tour the country and decide where to put down roots. Both of us had owned houses in the past and didn't miss the maintenance and upkeep. We thought of ourselves as minimalists. We lived at Pecan Grove for 15 years.

I had grown up in the suburbs of a northern city and never understood why we had to drive three miles for a quart of milk or why the infrequent buses stopped running late in the day and were missing in action on weekends. It was like living on a reservation, or in a segregated white middle-class enclave, or maybe in a kind of purdah for the '50s and '60s stay-at-home women I grew up with. Not that they necessarily minded living there, but, for an imaginative child, suburbia wasn't exactly inspiring.

Location was the strongest point. We were a mere seven-minute walk from the hike-and-bike trail, the Zachary Scott Theatre, convenience stores and restaurants. I could walk up Lamar and across the river to Whole Foods or nearby BookPeople in under half an hour or drive there in minutes.

Although we jokingly referred to ourselves as "trailer trash," I quickly learned to prevaricate when more upscale acquaintances asked where I lived. For a couple of years, I belonged to a book group that read Victorian

More than 130 residents live in South Austin's largest RV park, Pecan Grove, as condominium construction looms next door.

Author Diane Barnet and her husband William outside their Pecan Grove home of fifteen years.

novels. We met in a few members' homes, residences that resembled antique-filled, chintz-ruffled B&Bs or sumptuous villas in Tuscany. Whenever I was asked where I lived, I always replied "in South Austin." If I slipped and mentioned Barton Springs Road, eyebrows would shoot up quizzically. There were no actual houses on Barton Springs Road.

For a time I did some consulting and freelance writing from home. During one business phone call, rain was pelting down on the trailer's metal roof. "Your house must have a tin roof!" exclaimed my client delightedly. Little did he know. Another hazard was making business phone calls from my desk with the window open. A neighbor with a loud voice invariably would be bawling greetings to a friend or calling his dog as I tried to converse. I learned to close up before I dialed.

Most RVs and trailers are well kept, their cement patios enhanced by welcoming outdoor furniture, exotic plants, pottery, ollas and wind chimes. Elaborate gardens bloom on some sites. Many include small greenhouses and gazebos. One couple even had fishponds. Most of the nearby restaurants feature live music on their patios during the temperate months. The noise is fairly subdued, but you can always go inside and turn on the A/C to obliterate it, and it's finished by 11 p.m.

Matthew McConaughey and Others

Pecan Grove's residents have included retirees, musicians, wannabe writers, actors and artists, nurses, social workers, students of all ages, lobbyists, a judge, workers at nearby fast-food restaurants, a few people on social assistance and an ex-con or two. In 2006 actor Matthew McConaughey lived in the park for a few months in total privacy. Although a few neighbors chatted casually with him, there was no rush of autograph-seekers besieging his Airstream trailer. He used to stroll to the mailboxes wearing a ratty bathrobe, and greeted me with "Mornin', ma'am" on the few occasions our paths crossed.

While the park can be a refuge for the marginal, the quirky and the disaffected, most residents have middle-class values and are articulate and well informed on issues both local and international. For several years there were monthly summer potlucks under the huge old pecan trees, just like block parties or neighborhood barbecues in other types of neighborhoods. When there are bumper pecan harvests, residents collect huge sacks of nuts and can be seen crouching to harvest them throughout the park.

Residents often barter services or offer them for cash. A hairdresser cut hair on her days off. A writer edited a neighbor's manuscript in exchange for having his patio shrubs transplanted. A musician tuned a guitar and fixed computer glitches in return for lifts to the supermarket.

The park saw its share of gypsies. Sometimes an entire family of hippies, including two or three school-age kids, paused for a while. Touring musicians in battered, graffiti-covered vans or buses made occasional stops. One neighbor made a living as a clown, and often could be seen stopping at the community mailboxes in full regalia of fright wig, baggy pants and turned-up shoes. I wondered whether first-time visitors to the park thought she was a typical resident.

Another tenant, who lived in an old Winnebago near the laundry and shower block, regularly played yowling mariachi music in the evenings that was only too audible to anyone walking by. The occupant resembled an aging Elvis and could be truculent and taciturn, but once offered to let me use his ironing board in the laundry room. Reportedly a private investigator, he vacated his site in a huff after a dispute with management.

Given the strong sense of community, the park is a good place to be an elderly person living alone. Frail widows can always find someone to help move heavy flowerpots or power wash their trailer roofs. One aging widower was virtually adopted by a retired army officer neighbor who had a master's degree in languages and was also a practicing Buddhist. She checked on him frequently, making sure he was taking his medicine and eating properly. Her attention continued even after he went into a nursing home. During my park years, I drove two neighbors with chest pain and one with a suspected broken arm to the emergency room.

Just wandering through the park brings people into contact as they walk dogs, check for mail, schlep to the laundry room, showers or dumpster or stroll the perimeter for exercise. The sole Dumpster on the property is a magnet for abandoned but usable chairs, picture frames, plastic shelves and tools stacked around it. Often on Sunday mornings as I returned from buying the paper at the convenience store across the street, a skinny elderly black man would rise from the depths of the dumpster. We said "good morning" as though we were sedately walking dogs; dumpster diving was simply part of his lifestyle.

The Laundry Room and Vigilance

The laundry room is a sort of community clearing house. It has four washers and dryers and a table where residents can deposit unwanted items such as books, magazines, maps, small tools, bric-a-brac and even usable clothing. An avid recycler, I'm not too proud to admit that an obviously never-worn pair of dress pumps, designer jeans, a fake-suede skirt and a small handbag all found their way into my wardrobe. I still wear the skirt. One summer I hit a bonanza in the form of three brand-new discarded T-shirts and two pairs of shorts in my size, the pockets still sewn shut.

The laundry room bulletin board updates occupants on rules ("No tool sheds," "Pick up after your pets or else!"), holds notices of neighborhood association meetings and sometimes features semiliterate rants about parking space encroachments or litter violations.

Adjacent to the laundry room are concrete shower blocks for men and women. We tended to use them because they had better water pressure than our own tiny shower, but a few occupants of VW campers or the equivalent use the shower block out of necessity. Every few years, the showers are closed for a week or two for painting or maintenance, sparking a near panic as those without their own showers buddy up to neighbors or become extra resourceful at tracking down alternatives.

Dramatic events occur with enough frequency to provide a season's worth of soap opera episodes. A couple of drug busts took place during my residence, but they happened deep in the back of the park and I was blissfully unaware when they went down. A television crew planned to interview some residents for comments after one incident. An excited neighbor tipped me off, telling me I could actually appear on the evening news. "Uh, I don't think so, but thanks anyway," I responded cautiously, giving up the chance for my ten seconds of fame.

Occasionally, the park housed short-term tenants who happened to be on the lam. One day, two policemen with guns drawn cautiously approached the door of a trailer parked near us. The couple that had just moved in was having problems. He had threatened to come to her office and kill her, I learned later. No one was home when the police checked it out. I had never lived in a neighborhood where cops with weapons appeared out of nowhere. Fortunately, the couple soon split up and moved on.

For several years one neighbor persisted in sitting outside on his patio under a plastic tarp in all weather, his TV blaring, downing beers and arguing loudly with the occasional visitor. His site was diagonally opposite ours. When his nephew moved in, I became suspicious. The young man seemed to bear the stamp of a recent reform school graduate. Or was it simply my overactive imagination? Another neighbor, a skilled cabinetmaker, offered the nephew work as a helper. After he had to fire the nephew for non-performance, the erstwhile benefactor's tools disappeared.

Many neighbors complained about this neighbor over the years, but the manager always let him off with warnings. One night, his red-haired, Rubenesque live-out girlfriend, who was middle-aged and seemed far too intelligent and articulate for him, had a party at his trailer. Mercifully, we were away, but we heard plenty about it. To hear tell, this event featured dozens of loud, drunken women being chased around the park by Bubba-like males. After his long-overdue eviction, predictably carried out noisily over a period of several days, a couple of upended broken chairs and a scrawny plant were all that was left.

One night the sound of a revving motor woke me at 1 a.m. It was our neighbor's Ford 250 engine, parked six feet away from the window of our sleeping area. Someone must be sick, I reasoned. Maybe he was off to an all-night drugstore to get his wife some antihistamine tablets. In the morning the truck was gone. It was recovered in Tucson six weeks later. It hadn't helped that the keys had been left in the ignition, but the police detected a pattern. Expensive tools and lawn mowers had been removed from several other trucks in the park that night and stacked in neat piles beside them. It seemed the thief had concocted a plan to circle through the park, scooping up goodies he could fence. Something scared him off.

In my 15 years in the park, I experienced no thefts, other than a quilt that disappeared from a laundry room dryer the first year I lived there.

Vince, the skilled craftsman, wasn't so lucky. In addition to losing his tools, he had three new sets of jeans and denim shirts lifted from a dryer one day. It didn't seem to bother him. "I guess they needed them a whole lot more than I did," he said, and shrugged. Surprisingly few strangers or transients wandered through the park, especially after management locked the back gate.

Although there were homeless people and occasional panhandlers in the neighborhood, most seemed harmless. Only once, returning from my daily three-mile walk on the hike-and-bike trail, did an approaching passerby warn me that there was a belligerent drunk on the corner. I gave him a wide berth, actually crossing the street for half a block to avoid him.

Residents learned to be vigilant during special events at Zilker Park; the public is not above prowling the park for parking spots. On the other hand, some residents make money when there are crowds in the neighborhood. With Barton Springs Road closed off except for an emergency lane, a Pecan Grove writer set up a chair and table by the sidewalk where throngs walked by and sold a couple dozen copies of his self-published book of short stories set in the park.

Film Crews and the Yellow-Crested Night Heron

Film crews invaded Pecan Grove a couple of times to do segments for *Austin Stories,* a television series that aired briefly, and for a reality TV show that apparently never made it to the screen. The filmmakers attracted a few curious onlookers but probably sparked less interest than did the tree trimmers, who show up in summer with massive amounts of equipment.

We were also invaded over the course of two or three summers by the yellow-crested night heron. These large birds, drawn by the proximity of the river, like to fish at night. They built their nests high in the trees, preferably right above trailer roofs. At one point they had three huge nests located strategically around the park. After flying home with their catch, the herons proceeded to enjoy it, dropping slimy bones from a height of 40 feet. Small skeletal piles festooned RVs and littered the walkways. Ingestion of the prey resulted in droppings equally dramatic. The messy trailer roofs and slippery walks were collateral damage. High-powered water hoses were enlisted to destroy the nests, to little avail. One resident made the most of the situation by taking a series of zoom-lens photos of the herons and their habitats. The herons finally departed, leaving only the occasional possum or feral cat as specimens of urban wildlife.

Seven minutes from our trailer was the hike-and-bike trail along the south shore of Lady Bird Lake. It was backyard, nature preserve, meditation garden and so much more. To reach it, I turned left on Barton Springs Road, left at Jessie Street, crossed Toomey Road at the Zach Scott Theatre and cut through a parking lot adjacent to a city building. This brought me to the hiking trail by the river at a point where a small workout area attracted fitness enthusiasts who stretched their limbs and hung from raised bars. I made that walk thousands of times, almost daily, for fifteen years. I could have done it blindfolded or in my sleep.

West, along the south bank of the Colorado, the wooded trail comes to a quaint arched bridge over an inlet. From here, the sweeping view of downtown high-rises, luxuriant foliage, canoes and boats encompasses much that is best about the city. If you cross the bridge and turn right, another quarter-mile brings you to Lou Neff Point, a gazebo and lookout area. Nearby, ducks and a family of swans graciously accept breadcrumbs.

My walk took me another mile over the gently dipping and rising path, canopied by old trees, to the Mopac Bridge. Here, a concrete walkway below the bridge leads to the north side of the river. At this spot, running associations sometimes offer free water. I usually turned and went back the way I had come, covering three miles in a round-trip. It took me almost an hour of walking and an occasional break into a jog. Dedicated runners, joggers and speed-walkers passed me, but I overtook elderly bird-watchers and mothers pushing jogging strollers.

Sometimes I turned right after I crossed the Mopac Bridge and followed a more open trail hugging the north bank of the river. I passed a rowing club, broad wooden docks and an old stone tower. In season there are spring wildflowers in evidence here—bluebonnets, Indian Blanket, Texas Paintbrush. Taking this section of the trail means eventually crossing back to the south bank over a somewhat convoluted new foot bridge paralleling the Lamar Street bridge, from which foot traffic was banned after a series of accidents involving pedestrians occurred on its narrow sidewalks.

The trail seems almost an extension of Pecan Grove and the surrounding neighborhoods. It's one of the great amenities of living in South Austin.

SOUTH AUSTIN FROM THE BEGINNING

The broad Colorado River kept South Austin a collection of scattered farms through most of the nineteenth century. The action was north of the river, where in 1839 the settlement of Waterloo was renamed Austin and made capital of the Republic of Texas. For another ten years, anyone venturing south of the river risked an encounter with unfriendly Comanches.

For centuries Native Americans had camped and hunted in South Austin's lush woodlands, nourished by plentiful underground springs. Spaniards came through in 1709 on the Espinosa–Olivares–Aguirre Expedition, commemorated by a granite marker near the St. Edward's University entrance on South Congress Avenue. In 1730 South Austin became home to three Spanish missions displaced from East Texas. Frequent Indian attacks caused them to be moved a year later to San Antonio, where the missions are now known as Concepción, San Juan and Espada.

While Austin's prosperity continued as capital of the new state of Texas, the "ferry" established in the form of a free canoe left on the Colorado's north bank by William "Uncle Billy" Barton was upgraded to a boat by a Scotsman miller named John Grumbles. James Gibson Swisher from Tennessee moved his wife and four children to a farm atop a bluff south of the river in 1846. Five years later he started another ferry service, from the

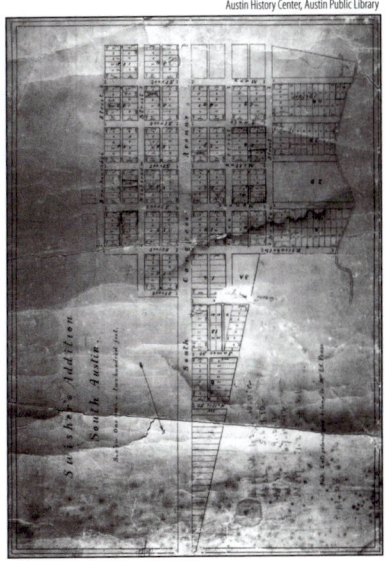

Austin History Center, Austin Public Library

South Austin's first platted subdivision was the Swisher Addition, created in 1877.

foot of Austin's Congress Avenue. Swisher also opened an inn and tavern nearby and donated a 120-foot-wide strip of land through his South Austin farm as a right-of-way for what became the main road between San Antonio and Austin, and the main axis for the Swisher Addition platted in 1877. In 1853 Travis County began setting rates for the growing number of ferry operators.

Swisher's Post Road or Old San Antonio Road became the forerunner of South Congress Avenue. Other dirt roads were evolving. Running south from the east–west Barton Springs Road that crossed the future South Congress Avenue were South First Street and Fredericksburg Road, now known as South Lamar Boulevard.

During the Civil War, the important road between Austin and San Antonio was defended in South Austin by the earthworks of Fort Magruder, built on the hilltop near the present northwest corner of South Congress Avenue and Ben White Boulevard. One of three forts built to protect Austin from a possible Union attack from the Texas coast, it was named for Gen. John Magruder, commander of the Confederacy's Texas forces.

South Austin's African American community grew following the Civil War. Former slaves stayed on to work for their former owners and others moved in. They formed communities in the Brackenridge Street neighborhood east of South Congress Avenue near Bouldin Creek—where they built St. Annie African Methodist Episcopal Church and Goodwill Baptist Church—and near South Lamar Boulevard and Kinney Avenue, building Barton Springs Baptist Church at 2107 Goodrich St. in the 1860s. Near the third church building on the site is a burial ground with six markers remaining with legible inscriptions. However, these and other African American communities throughout Austin were emptied in 1928

Goodwill Baptist Church at 1700 Newton St. is a survivor of the African American community near Bouldin Creek.

with the opening of a "Negro District" in East Austin, where the city made schools, parks and sewer lines available to African Americans only if they moved to the new district.

South Austin 's Hispanic community began increasing after the closing of Our Lady of Guadalupe Church in downtown Austin in 1926. By the 1940s, a small Hispanic population flourished around San José Church at the corner of West Mary and South 3rd Streets and expanded along South First and into the surrounding area.

With the end of the Civil War, access to the city north of the river began improving. In 1869 a pontoon bridge was built at the foot of Congress Avenue. It cost five cents to cross on foot and ten cents for a horse, exorbitant rates for that time. When a storm washed away the pontoons a year later, three different ferry services arose to brave the crossing. A wooden toll bridge was built in 1876, though in 1883 a herd of cattle stampeded across and the bridge collapsed. A cantilevered iron structure with a foundation of six stone piers and a wooden plank floor replaced the wooden bridge, though heavy tolls were still charged. A parade marked the opening of the first free bridge in 1886.

Scattered farm homes and then more pretentious Victorian homes marked South Austin through the latter 1870s, when sons of early settlers began subdividing their land. Eastward from South Congress Avenue came the Swisher Addition and the Bouldin Addition.

In 1887 the *Austin Daily Statesman* reported: "When the north side of the river is lined with factories, and the dense smoke of soft coal is resting like a pall over the city, then the South Side will become the main residence place. Mark the prediction."

Austin had remained in part a Wild West town of saloons and hitching posts, but it gained dignity in the 1880s with the founding of the University of Texas and construction of a new capitol building, its dome fourteen feet higher than that of the nation's capitol in Washington, D.C. In 1891 a new city charter tripled Austin's territory to 16.5 square miles, including South Austin. Joining the city brought water and electric lines to South Austin.

On South Congress Avenue, the Austin Motel occupies land that German immigrants Leonard and Frances Eck bought in 1888. The following year Eck started the first retail business south of the river, a general store in a two-story limestone building at 1200 S. Congress Ave. at the corner of Nellie Street. He soon diversified to include a pawnshop, livery stable and blacksmith shop, and acquired the first telephone south of the river. His daughter, Jennie Eck Stewart, inherited his properties in 1925 and opened other businesses along the block. By 1891 South Congress Avenue had eight buildings: the Eck building, two other houses, a log house, two grocery stores, a stonemason's shop and the J. M. Crawford & Company building, originally a grist mill at the corner of Elizabeth Street, where Güero's Restaurant now stands.

More formally planned subdivisions grew under the direction of Gen. William H. Stacy, who began Fairview Park east of Blunn Creek in 1880, and who would begin Travis Heights thirty-three years later.

Surviving in South Austin are three of Austin's Moonlight Towers, purchased for public lighting from the city of Detroit in 1894.

Austin gained public lighting in the form of thirty-one Moonlight Towers, bought from the city of Detroit in 1894. Each 165-foot tower had six carbon arc lamps illuminating a 1,500-foot-radius circle. Three towers survive in South Austin—at South First and Monroe, Leland Street at Eastside Drive and in Zilker Park—and now use mercury vapor lamps. Zilker Park's tower forms the core of the city's annual Christmas Tree, part of the park's Trail of Lights festival each December. Access across the river also improved, with completion in 1910 of the steel and concrete Congress Avenue Bridge. Streetcars in the new city system began rumbling across on a line extending south to Live Oak Street.

When America entered World War I in 1917, a flight training school was started at Penn Field, beyond St. Edward's University on South Congress. After the war, the University of Texas bought the land and built a radio school there but eventually sold the property to an industrial manufacturer.

During the 1920s, business expanded farther along South Congress, and hundreds of small bungalows sprang up in adjacent neighborhoods. Streetcars and automobiles had by then made commuting downtown to work easier. Today's Ben White Boulevard, was still called Allred Street, and caliche covered its surface.

Natural disasters interrupted growth, but only momentarily. A tornado in 1922 killed 13 people and damaged much of South Austin. A flood in 1935

Part of the South Congress Avenue bridge was under ten feet of water during flooding in 1935. The view, looking north, shows the state capitol at the end of the street.

submerged all of South First Street, the Congress Avenue bridge and part of South Congress Avenue under 10 feet of water. Floodwaters came onto the School for the Deaf grounds.

The Colorado's first dam was the 60-foot-high Austin Dam, built west of town in 1893 to create Lake McDonald, renamed Lake Austin. In 1900 the dam broke, resulting in serious flooding, deaths and loss of hydroelectric power. Rebuilding efforts culminated in another dam collapse. To reduce the nearly annual spring flooding, in 1934 the Lower Colorado River Authority was established and began supervising construction of a series of six dams, including Longhorn Crossing Dam (1960) to form Austin's Town Lake, since renamed Lady Bird Lake in honor of Lady Bird Johnson's conservation efforts in Austin and throughout the nation.

The 1928 City Plan that included storm sewers, zoning, street plans and much-needed paving throughout the city was expanded in 1930 to street paving, which included South Congress Avenue south to Oltorf Street. The South Austin Civic Association paved West Mary Street. Other neighborhoods followed suit. Depression-era WPA projects included Stacy Pool in Travis Heights and improvements to Deep Eddy pool west of Barton Springs. By the end of the decade, there were 10,000 people in

South Austin living in 2,360 homes, all served by the area's own newspaper, the *South Austin Advocate.*

As a major highway into Austin, South Congress became lined with highway billboards, motor courts, cabins, gas stations and restaurants. When the Terrace Motor Hotel opened on South Congress Avenue in 1950, it boasted the first motel swimming pool in town and 256 rooms, two pools, two restaurants and a banquet hall. Though business began declining somewhat when construction of IH-35 began in the 1940s, in 1952 the thoroughfare still had 21 motels and motor courts, 14 restaurants and hamburger stands, 12 gas stations, 9 building supply stores and the new state-of-the-art Twin Oaks Shopping Center near Oltorf Street.

Formal opening of IH-35 through Austin took place in 1962, slicing through the eastern edge of Travis Heights and orphaning, to the east, several blocks that become known as East Travis Heights. Public transportation links with the rest of the city, however, remained sketchy. As late as 1965, bus service south of the river stopped at dusk, leaving unsuspecting South Austin newcomers venturing downtown stranded there as evening fell.

As increased commercial competition created by the new IH-35 corridor caused business in South Austin to gradually decline, rents in South Austin became cheaper. During the '60s and '70s, South Austin became an alternative place for students to live, far from the fraternity and sorority houses around the stately University of Texas campus north of the river. A neighborhood off South First Street resonated with nighttime gunshots more often than not. Some of the typically modest one-story houses got barred windows while others flaunted barbed wire fences and vicious guard dogs. A small proportion of South Austin residents tolerated, consumed or dealt drugs. One quiet rundown residential street off South First beyond Oltorf was known as the Hippie Highway because dope could be bought there so easily. In South Austin, more than one superannuated musician has nodded out his later years in blissful obscurity, quietly maintaining habits developed in his glory days.

South of the Colorado, the homeless—pushing shopping carts from seedy motel to corner convenience store—were hassled less than they might have been downtown or even in East Austin. Ravines, creek beds and heavy foliage concealed squatters' camps, and petty crime increased. By the 1980s South Congress became known as an area of prostitution referred to as "the Strip," particularly the 1400 to 1600 blocks. Such activities inevitably spilled into adjacent neighborhoods.

Renovation of a rundown South Congress Avenue motel into the chic Hotel San José began in 1995, one sign of the increasing gentrification of South Austin.

Thanks to growing numbers of complaints and to more vigilant policing, however, by 1990 the worst appeared to be over, though seedy pockets remained. A few winos continued to consume bottles of Mad Dog at favorite corners. A few methadone clinics opened on South Congress beyond Oltorf. In 2001 South Lamar still had its share of porn shops, "lingerie modeling" studios, adult video shops, scruffy used car lots, auto repair businesses and laundromats. But gentrification was winning the day, as chic hotels and upscale restaurants and businesses opened in renovated buildings. Residential real estate prices soared, as classic but rundown bungalows were purchased and restored by young families. The trend was inevitably joined by high-rise condominium projects, though the number was kept down by fierce opposition to such projects from many neighbors.

New waves of arrivals didn't care that the Colorado had always been a socioeconomic dividing line, but memories of old South Austin persisted. Through the 1990s South Austin jokes featured refrigerators on porches, old cars raised on blocks in the front yard, blue-collar types drinking Pearl beer, chickens on the loose and trailer trash. South Austin was still called Bubbaville or the Used Auto Parts Capital of the World. Despite today's overwhelming gentrification, these memories live on in the folklore of the city.

BIBLIOGRAPHY

Barkley, Mary Starr. *History of Travis County and Austin, 1839–1899.* Austin: Austin Printing Co., 1981.

Boerner, Gerald. *Austin: 1836–1877.* Austin: Boerner, 1936.

Bright, Susan. *When the Streetcars Ran: An Oral History of Austin.* Austin: National Educational Laboratory, 1978.

Caran, S. Christopher. *Unique Areas in Austin, Texas.* Austin: Caran, 1974.

Cox, Mike. *Historic Austin: An Illustrated History.* Austin: Historical Publishing Network, 1998.

Erickson, Virginia. *Austin: The Past Still Present.* Austin: Austin Heritage Society, 1975.

Goldstein, Peggy. *At Home After 1840: Twenty-Seven Buildings in Austin, Texas.* Austin: Brick Row Book Shop, 1966.

Manaster, Jane. *The Ethnic Geography of Austin, Texas: 1875–1910.* Austin: Manaster, 1986.

Mays, Mitchell. *Stories and Tales of Green Pastures.* Austin: Mays, 1972.

_____. *The Blunn Family of South Austin.* Austin: Nichols, 1984.

Orum, Anthony M. Power, *Money and the People: The Making of Modern Austin.* Austin: Resource Publishing, 2002.

Parks, Bill. *Urban Growth in Austin, Texas: Causes, Consequences and the Future.* Austin: Regional Planning Program, University of Texas at Austin, 1984.

Reid, Jan. *The Improbable Rise of Redneck Rock.* Austin: University of Texas Press, 2004.

Shank, Barry. *Dissonant Identities: The Rock 'n' Roll Scene in Austin, Texas.* Lebanon, NH: Wesleyan University Press, 1994.

Shelton, Emmett. *My Austin: Remembering the Teens and Twenties.* Austin: American Press, 1994.

Spencer, Suzy. *Wasted.* New York: Kensington Publishing Corporation, 1998.

Thompson, Karen R. *Austin.* Mount Pleasant, S.C.: Arcadia Publishing, 2006.

Turley, Alan C. *Music in the City: A History of Austin Music.* Cedar Park, Tex: Duckling Publishing, 2000.

University of Texas Humanities Institute and Waterloo Press. *Writing Austin's Lives: A Community Portrait.* Austin. 2004.

Wassenich, Red. *Keep Austin Weird: A Guide to the Odd Side of Town.* Atglen, Pa: Schiffer Publishing, Ltd., 2007.

Weems, John Edward. *Austin, 1839–1989.* Austin: Austin American–Statesman, 1989.

Williamson, Roxanne Kuter. *Austin, Texas: An American Architectural History.* San Antonio: Trinity University Press, 1973.

Willoughby, Larry. *Austin: A Historic Portrait.* Virginia Beach, Va: Donning Publishing, 1997.

Woodruff, C. M. *Congress Avenue, Austin Texas: Lessons in Economic Geology, Architecture and History.* Austin: Austin Geological Society, 1988.

INDEX

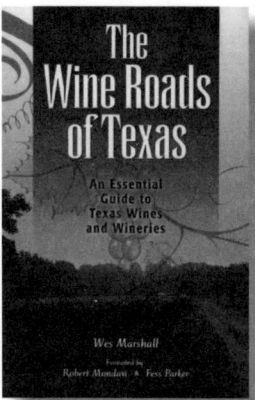